NIRP Research for Policy Series 10

Platforms for sustainable natural resource management:
the case of West Africa

C. Dangbégnon, A. Blum, E.S. Nederlof, N. Röling, and R.C. Tossou

Colophon

NIRP Research for Policy Series

Part 10: Platforms for sustainable natural resource management: the case of West Africa

The Netherlands-Israel Development Research Programme (NIRP) was established jointly by the governments of the Netherlands and Israel in May 1992 and coordinated through DGIS (Ministry of Foreign Affairs, The Hague) and MASHAV (the Centre for International Cooperation, Ministry of Foreign Affairs, Jerusalem). The Netherlands Government was the principal sponsor of the Programme, through Nuffic (the Netherlands Organisation for International Cooperation in Higher Education), until January 2001. During the period 2001-2003, the ongoing projects will be piloted towards administrative and scientific completion. The organisation and administration of NIRP are the responsibilities of Nuffic (The Hague) and Haigud (the Society for Transfer of Technology, Jerusalem).

Publication Board:
Prof. R.E. Isralowitz, Ben-Gurion University
Prof. L.W. Nauta, University of Groningen, the Netherlands (retired)
Dr. E.B. Zoomers, CEDLA, University of Amsterdam, the Netherlands

Mrs. M. Bar-Lev (Secretary)
CINADCO/Haigud
P.O. Box 30
Bet-Dagan 50200
Israel
Telephone: 972 - (0)3 9485441/9485
Fax: 972 - (0)3 9485761
E-mail: miriamb@moag.gov.il

L. Minkman (Project Officer)
CIRAN, Nuffic
P.O. Box 29777
2502 LT The Hague
The Netherlands
Telephone: 31 - (0)70 4260338
Fax 31 - (0)70 4260329
E-mail: lminkman@nuffic.nl

Published by:
Royal Tropical Institute
KIT Publishers
P.O. Box 95001
1090 HA Amsterdam
The Netherlands
Telephone: 31 - (0)20 5688272
Fax: 31 - (0)20 5688286
E-mail: publishers@kit.nl
Website: www.kit.nl

Text: C. Dangbégnon, A. Blum, E.S. Nederlof, N. Röling, and R.C. Tossou (edited by Mirjam A.F. Ros-Tonen)
Editor-in-Chief: Dr. Mirjam A.F. Ros-Tonen
Graphic design: Wil Agaatsz BNO, Meppel, the Netherlands
Printing: Veenstra, Groningen, the Netherlands

ISSN 1568-279X
ISBN 90 6832 6716
NUGI 124/651

Contents

4

Preface

The present booklet focuses on platforms for natural resource management. It analyses various cases in Benin and Burkina Faso where solutions need to be found for resource problems in conflictive and interdependent situations. The study involves various ecosystems, ranging from watersheds to rangelands and forests. By focusing on the interaction between stakeholders and social learning processes, the study is able to shed a light on the conditions for negotiated agreement and concerted actions in critical natural resource use situations. A team of researchers from Benin, Israel and the Netherlands carried out the study, the fieldwork of which was conducted in 1995, 1996 and 1997.

The study was funded by the Netherlands-Israel Development Research Programme (NIRP), which aims to encourage development-related research focused on socio-economic and cultural change. Being policy-oriented in nature, NIRP aims to make the results of research accessible to anyone interested in solving the problems investigated. The target groups for such knowledge include policy makers, representatives of non-governmental and donor organisations, and the scientific community. With this aim in mind, the Publication Board has launched the NIRP Research for Policy Series as a channel for the publication of "user-friendly" summaries of more than 30 scientific reports.

The Publication Board wishes to thank Dr. Mirjam A.F. Ros-Tonen for summarising the scientific report and editing this booklet. Thanks are also due to Mr. Robert R. Symonds for revising the English.

Last but not least, the Publication Board wishes to thank the research team for the successful completion of this study.

PUBLICATION BOARD:

Prof. Richard Isralowitz
Prof. Lolle Nauta
Dr. Annelies Zoomers

I. General information

I.1 Framework of the study

Benin, Burkina Faso and other countries in West Africa have faced serious environmental degradation during the last three decades. Natural calamities (such as droughts and inundation), capricious climatic conditions, inappropriate policies, wars, poverty and uncertainty about the world economic environment have further aggravated the situation. After the droughts of the 1970s and the 1980s, it became clear that resource depletion and human hardships and suffering are inextricably intertwined. The magnitude of the problem is so great that conventional public resources and services no longer suffice to prevent further degradation (Breemer, Bergh and Hesseling, 1995).

The awareness of this emerging ecological crisis has mobilised donors, governments, policy makers, researchers and development agents. They perceived the use of *gestion des terroirs* – a French approach to natural resource management – as a challenge to natural resource management and the solving of problems related to environmental degradation. This study analyses eight cases in six regions where such an approach was put into practice. These cases share a situation of problematic management of scarce and degraded natural resources on which farmers, herders, fishermen and hunters have to rely. The aim is to explore the conditions for negotiated agreement or concerted action in such critical natural resource use situations, where various stakeholders interact. The study starts from the assumption that the collective management of natural resources and the use of indigenous knowledge in participatory decision making can bring about an improvement in rural development intervention.

Four of the six sites under study were located in five provinces in the south and middle of the Republic of Benin (Atlantique, Mono, Couffo, Ouémé and Collines). Two sites were located in the Tuy and Houet Provinces of Burkina Faso (Figure 1). The six sites differ in natural resource systems, ethnic groups and management problems.

7

1. Lake Aheme, between the Mono and Atlantique provinces
Lake Aheme is located in the southern part of Benin and is partially a natural frontier between the Atlantic and the Mono provinces. Different peoples, who live in more than 40 villages around the lake, exploit the lake for its fish, shrimps and crabs. The two most important ethnic groups among the users are the Pedah and the Ayizo. The Pedah live on the western side of the lake and are dominant in some villages on the eastern side. The Ayizo live in the northern part, in Bopa (the western side) and in some important villages on the eastern side. The main problem in this region is the long-standing conflict over the fishing rights on Lake Aheme.

2. Rangeland management in the Collines province
In the *sous-préfectures* of Savè and Ouèssè in Collines province, along the frontier with Nigeria, live the Chabe people. The Chabe are cattle owners, farmers and hunters, who also engage in some border commerce activities, taking advantage of their geographical position. The Chabe use their indigenous organisations for the management of their natural resources. This case study focuses on the local arrangements for rangeland management.

3. Watershed management in two eco-zones in the province of Mono
This part of the study compares two regions with different peoples. The first is the densely populated Adja plateau, inhabited by the Adja people. The Adja are a homogeneous socio-cultural group, who originated in Togo and created several villages in the Couffo province. They practise a kind of intensive cultivation with inter-cropping, relay-cropping and indigenous agroforestry, based on oil palm trees. The Adja farmers practise minimum tillage, under which system weeds and crop refuse are left on the soil. The watershed problems in the Adja region consist of water erosion, decline of soil fertility, and the degradation of relic forests on hills in the upstream areas of watersheds. The second region is the *sous-préfecture* of Ouèssè (in the Collines province), which is dominated by the Mahi people. Their main activity is agriculture, practised as shifting cultivation. They do not use fertilisers, as a consequence of which the agro-ecological environment is being degraded through continuous land clearing.

4. Soil improvement by a women's group in Djeffa, Ouémé province
Djeffa is a densely populated coastal village in the southern part of the Ouémé Province in Benin. The dominant ethnic group in Djeffa is the Xla people. In the Djeffa area, the soils are poor in organic matter and infertile.

8

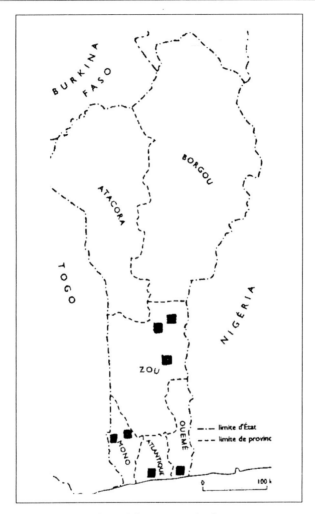

Figure 1 Location of the research sites

This case study focuses on a woman's group which set up a production cooperative. They developed an integrated system of activities to help produce organic matter to improve the stability and fertility of their soil for horticulture.

5. The Maro Forest in Tuy province, Burkina Faso
The Maro Forest is located in the south-western province of Tuy (formerly Houet), along the Bobo-Dioulasso–Dedougou road, about 75 km north-west of 9

Bobo-Dioulasso. It has an area of 56,227 hectares and it had a total population of about 40,000 in 1996. During the last few years, decentralisation and local participation have been introduced into the management of the Maro Forest. The population recognises this status and is willing to invest in managed afforestation. However, the people still regard the officially protected natural forest as an open access area, in which they chop trees illegally. The joint learning process, which led from centralisation to collective action, is still going on.

6. The Zone Sylvo-Pastorale in the Houet province, Burkina Faso
The zone covers the villages in the departments of Satiri and Bekuy and all the villages surrounding the Maro Forest in Tuy Province. The zone has an area of 2,029 km². As in Benin, the utilisation of the *terroir* (the villagers' land area) is characterised by serious conflicts between different categories of stakeholders – herders and farmers – who have clashing interests. The case study focuses on the *Programme National de Gestion des Terroirs* (PNGT); a government programme supporting the creation of a forest-pastoral zone through cooperation between international interests and local people and NGOs.

I.2   Objectives and research questions
Of the many problems of adaptive resource management faced by scientists, policy makers and practitioners, the most critical is how to intervene in the real world of resource use, which is characterised by conflicts, chaos, uncertainties and risks, in order to encourage regenerative practices in ecosystems and achieve sustainable development. Platforms for adaptive resource management form a possible approach to the problem. The main question addressed in this study is the extent to which the platforms for adaptive resource management help develop theories, practices and ideas in the particular contexts of resource use in Benin and Burkina Faso, for the facilitation of adaptive resource management.

The main purpose of this study is to explore the conditions for negotiated agreement or concerted action in critical natural resource use situations or through interactions between various stakeholders. In other words, this study focuses on the "soft side" (*cf.* Röling, 1997) of natural resource management.

The sub-objectives of this research can be stated as follows:
-    To analyse various resource management situations from Benin and Burkina Faso.

- To gain insight into the reason why some resource management situations are successful and others fail.
- To generate, from the ground, concrete theories, practices and strategies to support deliberate interventions for adaptive resource management.
- To make some practical recommendations for development.

Accordingly, the research questions deriving from the problem statement and objectives presented above, are:
- How can the various resource management situations from Benin and Burkina Faso best be analysed?
- What are the factors that affect the success or failure of the various resource management situations analysed?
- Can concrete and fresh theories, concepts and ideas be identified to support the facilitation of deliberate adaptive resource management interventions towards greater sustainability?

I.3   Hypotheses and methodology

The research was based on the "grounded theory", which is a way of building theory based on the empirical data from qualitative research (cf. Glaser and Strauss, 1967; Strauss and Corbin, 1990). Grounded theory principles concern the use of a systematic set of analytical induction, interpretation, comparison and coding procedures to develop a theory that is grounded in data collected in the real world. This means that the research does not start with a preconception of the reality through the definition of hypotheses derived from existing theories which are ultimately tested. Some concepts and ideas at the beginning of a study can be seen only as a guide to the exploratory research, although the finding – the theory – must be contextualised.

During the exploratory study, the grounded theory principles can offer the opportunity to acquire novel concepts, ideas, metaphors and methods which can be reiterated into the emerging relevant theory for adaptive resource management. Instead of using an existing theory or "truth" to explain (or understand) phenomena involved in adaptive resource management, it would be more useful to be creative and pragmatic about the way of going about this issue. To paraphrase Rap (1997: 7), one can argue that the intention is to look at the problems of resource management in their relation to societal problems from fresh, unprejudiced, sometimes counter-intuitive, yet well-founded, points of view and to call into question what appears self-evident.

11

The research methods and techniques applied in the case studies comprised unstructured and semi-structured interviews with carefully selected key informants, the snowball technique and life histories, participant observation, imaginative methods and techniques and the use of documents as additional sources of information.

A key informant could be an individual stakeholder, a representative of an interest coalition, an actor in a development or research organisation (governmental or non-governmental), a political or administrative representative, a representative of a funding organisation, etc. In most of the case studies, the snowball technique was used to identify the key informants for the interviews.[1] In using the snowball technique, particular attention was paid to stakeholders who had some particular duties, responsibilities or leading roles relating to resource management. A life-history approach was applied to this kind of stakeholders (*cf.* Pelto and Pelto, 1978).

In participant observation, the observer shares in the life activities and sentiments of people and his role reflects the social process of living in society (Bruyn, 1966). The delicacy of this task requires the observer to be tactful (Berreman, 1972). The hypothesis-generating ability of participant observation stems from the observer's ability to apply a theoretical perspective to his observations and to respond to both uniformities and regularities in what he sees. Theoretical richness is obtained through an analysis based upon the observer's frame of reference (Pelto and Pelto, 1978; McCall and Simmons, 1969; Peacock, 1986).

The principal researcher was in the field for all the case studies. This enabled him to observe both the stakeholders in their day-to-day activities (farming, fishing, cattle keeping, etc.), social events (conflicts, conflict resolution, meetings, collective activity) and the activities of professionals and researchers. According to Billaz and Diawara (1981: 112), it is in the field that the "rationality", the organising principle of what stakeholders do and think, can be understood.

Finally, relevant secondary documents were used as additional sources of information for the case studies. Examples of such documents are:
- government reports on general resource management policy;
- resource management project documents;

---

1 This method is a type of sampling procedure in which, for example, choosing one informant may generate information about other persons, which leads the observer to contact one of these others as a second informant. The second informant, in turn, directs him to a third informant etc., in an extensive chain of contacts (McCall and Simmons, 1969).

- consultancy reports;
- basic/applied and socio-economic reports; and
- historical documents which give a view of the past and present of a resource management process.

I.4   Theoretical framework

Below, we will first define the main concepts used in this study (Section I.4.1), after which we will elaborate upon resource management problems (Section I.4.2). As will be seen, the problems of resource use and management cover three dimensions: technical (ecosystems degradation), strategic (common good and public good dilemmas) and organisational (critical social events). This study takes collective action and platforms as the central conditions for effective sustainable natural resource management. To deal with the two different aspects (*i.e.* the social, or stakeholders, and the natural, or ecosystems), "coupled system thinking" was used to elaborate perspectives of natural resource management.

I.4.1   Definition of concepts

This study is mainly concerned with renewable natural and man-made ecosystems. *Ecosystems* refer to the structural and functional interrelationships among living organisms (plant, animals and microorganisms) and the physical environment within which they exist. A distinction can be made between fishery ecosystems, rangeland ecosystems, watershed ecosystems, forest ecosystems, etc. (Conway, 1986, 1994).

Ecosystems are open systems which transform inputs into outputs. Five elements can be distinguished in all ecosystems: inputs, components, interactions, cycling and boundaries. Components can be individual organisms in a population, or various populations in a biological community. Their arrangement defines the organising principles. Boundaries are not always clearly known and can be purposefully or opportunistically set. Ecosystems are empirical systems that must be described to understand the characteristics and the organising principles. Biodiversity and ecological services trigger the processes whereby inputs are transformed into outputs.

Biodiversity is defined as genetic, species and ecosystem diversity. Genetic and species diversity provide the units through which energy and materials flow, giving the ecosystem its functional properties (Constanza and Folke, 1996). Soil flora and fauna, for example, play a major role in many soil processes and soil-plant interactions, such as soil formation, biomass decomposition to humus and the uptake of nutrients by plant roots.

13

Ecological services are the tasks performed by the biotic and abiotic components of ecosystems for obtaining natural resources to supply human needs, such as fish, pasture, fodder, water and oxygen. Constanza and Folke (1996: 17) argue that ecological services include the maintenance of the composition of the atmosphere, amelioration of climate, provision of food, maintenance of species and a vast genetic "library", as well as maintenance of scenic landscape, recreational sites, and aesthetic and amenity values. In that view, ecological services are perceived to support human activities or affect human well-being.

Stakeholders, whether they are farmers, herders, fishers, agroforesters, horticulturalists or irrigators, are those who are directly concerned with the use of resources generated or available through ecosystems. They are engaged in various activities through which they interfere with or exploit resources in ecosystems for their subsistence. Stakeholders include all those who affect or are affected by the policies, decisions and critical events (collective impact of resource depletion) affecting the ecosystem under siege. Stakeholders can be identified on the basis of their interests in the ecosystem under siege, the practices they use and the type of rights, responsibilities and duties they have. Stakeholders appropriate natural resources for their livelihood.

In this study, the concept of *natural resource* means all kinds of goods which stakeholders appropriate from ecosystems for their livelihood. This appropriation by one stakeholder creates a diminution for the others. In concrete terms, fish stock harvested by one is not there for someone else. As such, these natural resources can be considered as *common pool resources*.

There are also natural resources characterised by joint use, which means that their use does not create a diminution for others. Examples are air, oxygen and forest beauty. Infrastructures such as irrigation canals, firebreaks and other features that help to exploit common goods are also characterised by joint use. Goods characterised by joint use are considered in this study as *public goods*.

Resources concern both common pool resources and public goods. *Resource use* means the appropriation of goods from ecosystems (for example, fish stock).

Regenerative practices are applied ecological principles and all kinds of measures and actions that work to restore the productivity, functioning, resilience and continuity of ecosystems. Measures and actions can be based on socio-economic, political or cultural principles. Examples are the rationing of the use of natural resources (especially common goods) and involving local organisations in decision making on the environment.

I.4.2   Framing the problems of resource management
The problem of resource management can be framed as having three
dimensions: (i) the use of scarce natural resources; (ii) degradation of
ecosystems and critical events; and (iii) the maintenance of ecosystems in
good health.

(i) The problem of natural resource scarcity and stakeholders' behaviour
Problems with natural resource scarcity arise where the joint use of
ecosystems and subtractive benefits are coupled with scarcity, and where, in
consequence, joint users start to interfere with each other's use (*cf.* Wade,
1988: 184). In their use of scarce natural resources, stakeholders will face the
problem of resource flow allocation in a competitive arena (Ostrom, 1990).
Hardin (1968) predicts the "tragedy of the commons" in such situations,
where stakeholders have complete freedom and there is no control over the
access to the ecosystems which hold scarce common goods. The challenge for
resource management may be the extent to which the problem of common
goods dilemmas is overcome, with stakeholders agreeing to *take less* through
collective choice. Stakeholders can generate rules and regulations and
cooperate for successful collective action (*e.g.* McCay and Acheson, 1987; Wade,
1988; Warren, 1991; Mckean, 1992). However, a systematic process, which
generates a prospect of solution through communication, is now emerging
(*e.g.* Röling, 1994 a and b, 1996). Within a communicative approach, overcoming
common goods dilemmas would involve stakeholders realising the collective
negative effect of individual actions and agreeing to cooperate and ration the
use of common goods.

     In addition to common good dilemmas, there is also the *assurance problem*,
which means that stakeholders, in the face of the scarcity of resource flow
allocation, may change their behaviour and adopt individual actions instead
of following the agreement made for collective choice. They do so because
they do not have the complete assurance that the others are respecting the
rules and regulations (Sen, 1967). Assurance may also be obtained through
reliance on formal policy, formal surveillance and the effectiveness of a
punishment structure (*cf.* Ostrom, 1990).

(ii) The problem of ecosystem degradation and/or critical events
Ecosystem degradation and/or critical social events surrounding resource
use are environmental problems which have technological and social
dimensions. An environmental problem can be defined as any change of
state at the ecosystem level (Sloep, 1994).This change of state may result
firstly from the degradation of the structure of the ecosystems, for instance,   15

through loss of keystone species, habitat degradation or depletion of common goods (De Groot, 1992). This endangers ecological services and the functioning of biodiversity. Secondly, it may result from abiotic factors (such as water and air pollution or the adverse effects of drastic climatic change) and from biotic factors. An example of the latter is the emergence of a new ecological order, such as water hyacinth, and its harmful consequences for water resources.

An environmental problem may also be any critical event such as the emergence of a difficult state of affairs, debate and paradox about resource use among stakeholders. These concerns refer to the impacts of current individual practices on ecosystems, as well as to collective negative societal impact. Some concrete examples of such problems are roaming animals and crop damage by cattle, conflict and war over resource use, and impasses over concerted action for resource use.

Environmental problems such as those described above can be effectively considered as problems to be dealt with, only if they are widely shared. Their perception depends on the existing frames of reference, belief systems and norms of stakeholders (Breemer et al., 1995: 103-4), and of those who intervene or have the task of dealing with a problem. Stakeholders might not perceive soil erosion to be a problem even where technical surveys have made it plausible that there is one. The problem needs to be socially constructed in relation to existing (micro and macro) economic opportunities, strategic reasoning and the conception of ecosystem assets by the stakeholders. In empirical situations, it seems relevant to adopt an interpretative approach to the perception of the problem by various stakeholders and other actors (researchers, development workers, policy makers) in governmental and non-governmental development organisations.

(iii) The problem of provisions for the maintenance of ecosystems and coordinated action

In the present study, provisions are defined as contributions in terms of money, labour, know-how, innovations, responsibility assignment and credible commitment. Provisions also call for solidarity, which is the willingness to sacrifice resources (mechanic solidarity) or immediate gratification for the welfare of others (organic solidarity), out of the feeling of unity. Provisions are directed to improvements, infrastructures and coordinated actions for maintaining ecosystems in good health, as well as for the well-being of stakeholders. *Improvements* are all kinds of efforts that contribute to enhancing, strengthening or creating ecological services to regenerate natural resources and or maintain the functions of ecosystems. Concrete examples of such types of improvement are the production of organic matter, afforestation, or the reconstitution of mangrove stands for restoring fishponds. *Infrastructures* are different kinds of structures which form part of the ecosystems and help to maintain them in a good health or prevent them from being destroyed by environmental factors. Examples of such kinds of infrastructure are firebreaks and gullies for erosion control. There are also infrastructures which make possible the exploitation of natural resources. Canalisation infrastructure for irrigation is an example of this type. Long-term *coordinated actions* are required for maintenance and governability. Provisions, in this context, are defined in terms of responsibility assignment, credible commitment and mutual monitoring for sustaining organisations that govern resource use or coordinate and monitor investments and provisions needed for the improvement and the maintenance of infrastructures. In situations where scarcity does not apply to the use of common goods, governing organisations and institutions will be needed or maintained for anticipating scarcity in the future.

Improvements, infrastructures and organisations for coordinated actions define public goods situations which offer free-riding incentives, *i.e.* the opportunity to benefit without making any contribution. For example, investments in the reconstitution of a mangrove stand for the improvement of the productivity of a lake fishery will benefit all the fishing community, including those who did not contribute. The motivation to free ride, or to contribute too little, may increase since people can enjoy their share of the benefits without contributing to them (Olson, 1978). Such situations are described in terms of *public goods dilemmas*: the choice between "give some" or free ride (Dawes, 1980).

The challenge for resource management seems to be the extent to which the problems of public goods dilemmas are overcome, which means that stakeholders agree to *give more* for the provisions. But, the metaphor "*give more*" can work only if the voluntary collective action of stakeholders is effective. The resource management problem then becomes how to maintain the facilitation of voluntary collective action for the provision of public goods.

Synthesis: the nature of the problems and the puzzles for resource management
The problems of natural resource scarcity and provisions can be solved if common goods and public goods dilemmas are overcome, which means that stakeholders must agree on *take less* and *give more*. Ecosystem degradation and/or critical social events affecting resource use may be perceived differently by stakeholders and interventionists and can then be solved if there is a shared understanding about collective responses. It seems that

solutions to the different problems will be possible only if successful collective action is effective and individual actions are consistent with collective action. Organisations, be they local, governmental or non-governmental, are groups of individuals with common objectives. They mobilise resources (money, staff, facilities), perceive objectives and policies (e.g. existing government plans), deliver strategies, and use societal norms to legitimate a process of change. Organisations also provide a structure for human interaction. A distinction can be made between local organisations which are created by the stakeholders themselves, and organisations created by the government (extension organisations, for example) or outside the local setting.

The first dilemma of resource management therefore concerns *collective action*: who or what triggers or maintains collective action among stakeholders and to what extent can the facilitation of successful collective action be effective?

The second dilemma of effective resource management can be defined in terms of structural arrangements or *platforms*. The main question here is at what level(s) of aggregation of stakeholders and levels of the ecosystem are responses effective. Platforms for natural resource management (Röling, 1994c, 1995; Röling and Jiggins, 1998) are based on soft systems thinking[2] and emphasise the need to create a collective agency at a level of social aggregation commensurate with the ecosystems level at which present sustainability problems are deemed manageable. The idea that a natural resource requires a platform to manage it sustainably, leads to coupled systems thinking (Röling, 1997). This is an attempt to integrate hard and soft system thinking in order to analyse how interventions can be directed for solving resource management problems in the complex natural and social worlds.

I.5   Elaboration of the research

The perspective of coupled system thinking makes it possible to develop the notions of platform and social learning to cope with both ecosystem and

---

[2] System thinking is a way of looking at reality, organising knowledge, orienting data collection and directing intervention in complex phenomena and social arenas (Checkland, 1981; Fresco, 1986; Engel, 1997). This study used coupled systems thinking to elaborate perspectives of resource management. Coupled systems thinking comprises "hard system thinking" and "soft system thinking". The first is applied to conceptualise ecosystems for the purpose of resource management. "Soft system thinking" is applied as a way of organising our attempt to reach a common appreciation of problematic situations. See Dangbégnon (1998) for a further discussion of these approaches.

social dynamics, and to facilitate change in resource management through communicative intervention, incentives, support institutions and policy contexts (see Dangbégnon (1998) for further details). These notions suggest that adaptive responses can provide novel solutions to evolving conditions. Thus, adaptive, rather than straight, resource management is concerned with the integration of social dynamics into the "facilitation" of change. The elaboration of the concept of adaptive resource management is one of the objectives of this study.

In the present study, analytical paths are elaborated which seem to be relevant for the analysis and comparison of the data from the case studies. The identification of a common pattern of variations for the issue under investigation is considered as a starting point for building an analytical framework. Temporal and spatial variations at the levels of the ecosystems and the social dynamics of the stakeholders are important for the adaptive resource management perspective. Here, the consideration of the temporal and spatial variables in the path would seem to be a precondition for ensuring rigour in the inquiry. Two analytical paths are considered: the first follows a temporal variation of the case study and the second focuses on sub-case studies which present spatially different characteristics of a case.

In the first analytical path (temporal variations) the study proceeded as follows:
-   The definition of time scales according to some perceived events or assumptions which seemed to be relevant for the changing patterns of the case study in terms of the problems of resource management.
-   The description of the ecosystem under siege and identification of the stakeholders at the time of the study.
-   The pursuit of the analysis through the time scales, using the key variables in the perspectives for adaptive resource management: the problems, the social learning, and the facilitation of changes.
-   The drawing of conclusions, through a retrospective look at the data, about the nature of the platform(s) and the assessment of greater sustainability.
Four case studies follow this analytical path: the Lake Aheme, the Djeffa women, the forest-pastoral zone and the Maro Forest.

In the second analytical path (spatial variations) the study proceeded as follows:
-   Making visible the variables which constitute the ground of the spatial variation of the case study in several sub-case studies, taking into

19

consideration how the resource management problems of the sub-cases are related.
- Using the key variables in the perspectives for adaptive resource management: the ecosystem and the stakeholders, the problems, social learning, the facilitation of changes and the nature of platform.
- Comparing the sub-case studies (mainly the differences) and providing a synthesis and a specific conclusion.

This analytical path was followed in the case studies of rangeland resource management and watershed management.

II. Results

II.1   The development of platforms for the resource management of Lake Aheme

II.1.1   The ecosystem and stakeholders of Lake Aheme

Lake Aheme, in the southern part of Benin, has many economically valuable natural resources. Its fish species, called (in Pedah) *akpavi, guessou, siko, nongban, blolo* and *ahouè* are highly appreciated in the markets (see Table 1). Other species like *degon, asson* and *todan* (shrimp, crab and eel) also have a very high economic value.

Table 1 Examples of Lake Aheme's fishery resources with important economic value according to the stakeholders

Local name (Pedah)	Scientific name
Akpavi (fish)	Sarotherodon melanotheron
Guessou (fish)	Mugil cephalus
Siko (fish)	Polynemus quadrifilis
Nongban (fish)	Elops lacerta
Blolo (fish)	Chrysichthys migrodigitatus
Ahouè (fish)	Ethmalosa fimbriata
Degon (shrimp)	Penaeus duorarum
Asson (crab)	Callinectes latimanus
Todan (eel)	Myrophus punctutus

Source: This study and Pliya (1980).

The main ethnic groups around the lake who exploit the resources – the Pedah and Aizo – share similar cultural patterns, beliefs and religious practices, and their languages are similar as well. Economically, they differ in that the Pedah are primarily fishers, while the Ayizo are also farmers. However, both ethnic groups hold a stake in Lake Aheme and may have different voices and interests.

An important source of conflict is the use of fishing practices called *xha* and *akaja*. Xha is a kind of fishing barrier installed at the southern part of the lake, which enables the owner to catch shrimps and fish species which migrate from the sea. The akaja system is a fishing device based on the principle of setting dense masses of branches in shallow water. This attracts a large number of fish because of its resemblance to the mangrove in providing shelter, refuge, shade and food for the lake's species. This fishing device is used in the central and northern parts of the lake. The owner of the akaja is the only one who is entitled to appropriate, after a certain period (6-12 months), the fish catches in this device.

The xha and akaja enable a few stakeholders to catch more fish, shrimps, crabs, etc. in Lake Aheme. Most other stakeholders catch few fish and become frustrated, which leads them to use fishing methods and equipment which are perceived as one of the causes of the depletion of the lake.

If Lake Aheme is to be used in a concerted manner, an agreement among the different groups of stakeholders seems to be the only way to achieve a solution covering the whole lake. In the following sections, the evolution of the problems, the learning processes, the facilitation of change, the management practices and the platforms for resource management are placed in a historical perspective. Four periods are distinguished: pre-colonial times before 1894, the colonial period (1894-1960), post-colonial times (1960-1990) and the era of democratisation after 1990. Using this historical approach, specific conclusions will be drawn about the extent to which greater sustainability is being achieved and the factors involved in successes or failures of fishery resource use. Emphasis will be placed on how different categories of the stakeholders, institutions and the organisation for governing the lake have emerged, how they interact and how they seek solutions for the problems of the lake.

II.1.2   Lake Aheme during pre-colonial times (before 1894)

Under the chaotic circumstances of tribal wars and migrations, the basic problem in the pre-colonial period was how to ensure subsistence for all the people. The lake, which was also used as a natural protection against enemies, was governed by an indigenous organisation consisting of King Zounon and the local priests. Their control over the lake was based on spiritual beliefs in voodoos (representations of God), like *Dagboehounsou*, which were perceived as the protectors of the lake and the stakeholders. The people feared this spirit might punish them if they did not follow its will, as interpreted by the priests. This ensured the collective use of the fishery resources according to a set of local rules. These were:

- the *djêtowlé* (jumping in the lake) was forbidden in order to protect the spawning ground of the fish;
- the *dobou-doboui* (chasing the fish by hand towards the fishing net in the water) was forbidden;
- the use of *mandovi* (a fishing net with a small mesh) and *djohoun* (a fishing tool with a lot of hooks) were forbidden;
- the fishermen were not allowed to practise fishing two days per week;
- fishing activities were not allowed during the period of the cult for the voodoos protecting the lake (usually 5-7 days);
- only King Zounon and his people were allowed to use the xha, the fishing barrier at the outlet of the lake, as a means of support for the kingdom.

Voodoo thus played an important role in the organisation of the stakeholders and the facilitation of successful decision making about the lake. The platform of stakeholders chaired by King Zounon brought all the stakeholders on the lake together for the effective management of its resources. Severe religious sanctions, embedded in the spiritual world, worked to ensure compliance. It could be said that magic and witchcraft created fears and reinforced trust of the local organisation which governed the lake. Messages to the stakeholders were perceived as sacred acts, with the function of informing them about the new norms and rules of the local institutions of the lake. The fact that King Zounon was the only one who was allowed to use the xha under the local arrangements, seemed to be a great incentive. This could also be interpreted as a way of sustaining the effectiveness of the local organisation and encouraging the stakeholders to maintain trust in the local institutions of the lake.

II.1.3   Lake Aheme during colonial times: 1894-1960
During the colonial period, the growing fishing community and market opportunities brought about increasing pressure on the lake, at a time when the population around the lake was increasing and indigenous organisation was being weakened. The lake was depleted and fishermen suffered. Individual interests became more important than adherence to the traditional rules. The problem was further aggravated because the mangroves, where the fish could breed in safety among the roots, were cut by the people and the ecological conditions of the lake were degraded (*cf.* also Pliya, 1980: 143). In response, the Fishery Service introduced the akaja (see Section II.1.1) to increase the productivity of the lake for all the fishermen. Originally, only the fishery service was supposed to manage the akaja, but with the destruction of the local organisation for governing the lake and the absence

23

of instruments to enforce sanctions, the fishermen started to use akaja freely. As stated above, the fishermen who use xha or akaja get more fish from the lake, while the majority of other stakeholders catch little or nothing. The xha users, who had once controlled the whole lake, regarded the lake as their property, but the other fishers considered it common property. Conflicts between clashing interest coalitions occurred. Various attempts by local mediators and government officials (who did not have much power) failed to solve the problem. Reciprocal destruction of the adversary's devices even led to fatal incidents.

By seeking a technological solution to the problems of Lake Aheme, the *Service des Pêches* did not perceive the importance of the social organisation of the stakeholders. The introduction of the akaja should have been complemented with training of the stakeholders in mutual monitoring and self-evaluation of the situation in their lake, and the raising of awareness of the need to agree on new behaviour to avoid the depletion of the lake.

Another problem affecting the effectiveness of the akaja in Lake Aheme was the absence of incentives for maintaining the akaja in good condition and exploiting it collectively. The individual economic interest dominated, and the stakeholders did not perceive the collective consequences of the impact of their individual fishing practices. They did not realise that they should maintain the local organisation for the governance of the lake. Nevertheless, despite the individual economic interest of the stakeholders, a platform should not be conceived only at their level. Other actors at a higher level of social aggregation than the lake are needed to mediate disputes and take decisions on new ways of using the lake. The *Service des Pêches* probably did not perceive the importance of this issue in acting to strengthen the existing local platform for the lake.

II.1.4   Lake Aheme after the independence of Benin: 1960-1990
In the post-colonial period, the use of both xha and akaja expanded. With the modification of local institutions, not only King Zounon, but also the relatives of the Zounon family could use the xha. The number of xha lines increased from 20 during the old times to 100 in 1975. This changing situation in the southern part of the lake led to the emergence of the Xha people.

At the same time, the failure of the *Service des Pêches* to organise the stakeholders at the beginning of the 1960s encouraged the growth of akaja to some 2,600 in 1969 (Welcome in Pliya, 1980: 145). Merchants, capitalists in the cities, and administrative bureaucrats were attracted by the akaja and provided some stakeholders with financial means to build them. The catches were shared between the outsiders and the stakeholder. Conflicts and fights emerged, as some stakeholders caught fish clandestinely in akaja which did not belong to them. Moreover, the increase in individual catches endangered the Lake Aheme ecosystem. The fishing effort[3] increased, but not the size of the catches. This is perceived as a sign of the degradation of the lake.

Beginning in 1964, several government initiatives were taken to improve the situation, including the establishment of the fishing police and the introduction of a kind of local aquaculture, called *hwédo*.[4] However, the introduction of hwédo failed, as the project did not cover all the stakeholders at the lake. The aquaculture was introduced only on the eastern side of the lake (the Atlantic province), while the western side (the Mono province) was not covered by any such project.

Finally, the Xha people took the initiative of creating a platform for collective decision making on the collective use of fishery resources. They realised the need to have an organisation at the level of the whole lake, as existed during pre-colonial times. Although they effectively established such platform, with representatives of each village around the lake and a set of laws, regulations and sanctions, their initiative eventually failed. The weakness of their organisation was that the akaja users were excluded. From that point of view, their organisation solved only the half of the problem of having an organisation at the level of the lake, because the akaja users formed an important coalition. Moreover, the context has changed and the Xha people were wrong to believe that the way the lake was governed during the pre-colonial period could be reproduced.

II.1.5 Lake Aheme in the democratisation era after 1990

During the democratisation era, when Benin adopted a new multiparty system, making decisions on the use of the lake became very difficult from a political point of view. Many attempts to solve the problems were not

---

3 Professionals use the concept of fishing effort as an indicator to explain the changing patterns of the physical use of the lake. The fishing effort is defined in relation to the changes in the tools used by the stakeholders. The fishing effort increases when more powerful tools – e.g. fishing nets with a smaller mesh size – are used.

4 The principle of *hwédo* is that the floodplain of the River Ouémé is flooded for at least four months each year and that both the plain and the river support fisheries based upon natural stocks. During the dry season, the plain is left dry and used for agriculture and grazing cattle. The fish population is confined to the main river channel and to a series of artificial ponds – the hwédo – dug by the stakeholders on the floodplain. A small channel drains the water of the lake into the hwédo. The fry are obtained from nurseries and raised in the hwédo. The small channel which communicates with the lake is closed to avoid fish moving to the lake. The type of fish used for the hwédo is *tilapia*, which is well appreciated in the Benin markets.

25

successful and always led to impasses. The frustrations of the fishermen had political consequences for those ruling the country (loss of votes). The politicians exploited the difficult situation of the stakeholders during their campaigns and used the organisations of the fishermen (akaja users and xha users) for their own purposes. When the government decided to do something about the lake (*e.g.* remove akaja and xha), the opponents would promise to re-establish them in exchange for votes. Moreover, the roles of the different categories of representatives (*e.g.* professionals, political authorities) in the platform, which was created by the government in 1992, were unclear. The weakness of the government in enforcing the actions that were implemented did not provide any incentive for the stakeholders to change their practices on the lake. Against this background, the main problem was to find strategies for breaking the impasse. In fact, the stakeholders had no choice but to find the solutions to their problems collectively and reduce the adverse consequences of their individual actions on the lake.

II.1.6   Lessons to be learnt from the Aheme Lake case
The analysis of fishery resource use in Lake Aheme shows how the effective platform for resource management has evolved since the pre-colonial period. The Lake Aheme case illustrates the dynamics of the lake's problems, and the institutions and organisations for its management. Moreover, the multiple stakeholders' responses to various interventions and changing patterns of policy contexts have been dynamic from the pre-colonial period to the recent democratisation period in Benin. The platform for resource management was successful before the impasses emerged. This situation presents a strong basis for drawing some conclusions about the factors that affect the success or failure of resource management on Lake Aheme.

A major factor ensuring the success of the management of the lake's resources during the pre-colonial time was that the stakeholders agreed upon a platform for governing Lake Aheme. Other related factors for success were the functioning of the institutions, existing local monitoring systems, periodic meetings of the local organisation for decision making and deliberation and the effectiveness of sanctioning structures. However, the success was achieved in a context for ensuring the subsistence of the stakeholders. The local arrangement failed beyond this context. The problems of the lake moved to the levels of external supports and policy, which failed to solve them.

Factors related to the failure were the difficulty of setting up new institutions for the lake and enforcing their decisions. Inconsistent policy frameworks did not allow concrete actions like facilitating the development of a new organisation among the interest coalitions that emerged, training the stakeholders to deal with the ecological problems of the lake, or creating a committee to start a learning process among the stakeholders. These processes require communicative professionals and a clear institutional framework, and both were lacking.

The major lesson from Lake Aheme is that, beyond technical measures for manipulating the ecology of the lake towards higher productivity (e.g. akaja, hwédo), and beyond biophysical studies to monitor the ecological state of the lake, greater sustainability can be achieved only if the stakeholders agree upon management rules (institutions), governing organisations and policies.

II.2   Platforms for rangeland resource management with Chabe people in Benin

The second case study deals with concrete resource management problems and efforts to solve them in rangeland ecosystems. Some special issues addressed in this study are the difficulty of identifying the boundaries of rangeland ecosystems, uncertainty about the movements of the herders to make best use of the heterogeneous landscape, and the risk of serious crop damage and conflicts and wars. The study was carried out in a region where the Chabe people are the dominant ethnic group. They are well organised around their local kingdom. The Oba is the King of all Chabe and is the highest authority living in Savè, the capital of the sous-préfecture. At the level of a Chabe village, the balodè is the local authority for the hunters and responsible for the protection of natural resources (forest resources, game, etc.). Each Chabe village also has a chief called balè ("the father of land"). He is responsible for the redistribution of farming land among the villagers. The balè governs the village with help of the baba balè (father of the balè) and the iya balè (mother of the balè) and other influential people. Land is under control of a native Chabe, called the agani (the land landowner). In sum, the Chabe use their indigenous organisations for the management of their natural resources.

The availability of land in Savè and Ouèssè and the socio-political organisation of the Chabe people enabled farmers and herders to settle in their territory. Several migrant farmers borrowed land from the agani. The transhumant herders also obtained permission to settle in the same area. The region attracts many herders because of the abundance of rivers and pastures. For instance, out of 185,600 hectares of cultivated land available, only 6% was used in 1989. Many ethnic groups (Adja, Fon, Otamari, Berba, etc.) migrated from the southern and the northern parts of Benin to the territory of the Chabe people. In the driest month, herders from the region of Ilorin in Nigeria also move into the region (transhumance).[5] Grazing areas and farmlands are intertwined.

Two different situations were investigated for this case study. The first situation concerns the settlement of herders and migrant farmers in an area used for grazing and cultivation. These stakeholders are using land that does not belong to them. The *agani* played an important role in their access to land and pasture. The herders and migrant farmers live in hamlets – called *gaa* by the native Chabe and *gure* in the herders' dialect – without any geographical, socio-economic or political centre. The socio-economic and political central functions are performed by the villages of the migrant farmers to which one or several hamlets of the herders are attached. This case study comprises three villages: Dani, Katakou and Ayedjoco.

The second situation concerns the local organisation of the Chabe people at the village level. The *balè* and *balodè* make the decisions about the settlement of the herders. Both native Chabe and herders use the village territory for their different activities: crop cultivation and herding. The village under study – Kemon – received external support for developing a platform for collective rangeland resource management.

II.2.1 Platforms for rangeland resource management under the local arrangement in the Savè area

The first case study of rangeland management focuses on the local arrangements made for the complex rangeland management in some villages of the *sous-préfecture* of Savè in the Collines province. Herders and other migrating people moved into the area with their herds after receiving permission from the *agani* (Chabe land owners). The herders exploit as pasture the same natural areas which are used by the farmers for cultivation. The cattle sometimes seriously damage the crops and conflicts between the farmers and the herders occur frequently.

The herders complained about the difficulty of sharing the same area with the crop farmers. The immediate problems perceived by them were the eating of crops by the cattle, the farmers' disrespect for the corridor space, the difficulty of gaining access to the watering places during the rainy season and the difficulty of finding water for the cattle during the dry season.

---

5   Transhumance can be defined as the seasonal movement of herders between different pastures.

The herders regarded the farmers' activities as a restraint on animal raising because it is difficult to move the cattle without damaging the crops when the crops are everywhere.

According to the villagers (the farmers), herding was a constraint on their farming activities, because of serious crop damage caused by the cattle. The most critical problem was the insecurity caused by the *transhumant* Fulbe[6] (the *buzu*) who are well equipped with guns. Another problem was the practice of lighting early bush fires by the herders, which hardens the soils and makes them difficult to cultivate.[7] In one of the villages (Ayedjoco) not all of the farmers perceived the herders as the main constraint on crop cultivation, because the herders were keeping their cattle. Here, the problem was related to the shifting cultivation practised by some migrant farmers. These migrant farmers did not respect the agreement between the village and the herders and were cultivating in the direction of the *gaa*, where the cattle damaged their cotton crops.

The context of Savè was characterised by the absence of a useful intervention to solve the problems which were identified. The many concrete problems of the herders – water, pastures, corridor space, etc. – cannot be solved without the cooperation of the other stakeholders, the migrant farmers and the *agani* in Savè. The land degradation, crop damage and conflicts which the farmers perceived could be reduced only if the various stakeholders reached a negotiated agreement, adopted collective action and created platforms to overcome the barriers they faced.

Stakeholders themselves sought for alternative solutions to these problems through local arrangements. The *balè* and the *agani* became active in the negotiations and mediation between herders and farmers. Several examples of collective rangeland management by the local organisations were noted, which reveal the importance of coalitions and networking, collective action, negotiated agreement with the villagers and external support. One of the examples was the negotiation by the herders in Dani for the use of clean water for the cattle. Another example was the attempt of villagers and herders to reach a negotiated agreement for herding and cultivation in Ayedjoco. Maintaining this negotiated agreement stimulated the development of a platform where the potential stakeholders became the

---

6   Herders are also called Fulbe. The singular is Fulani.
7   Lighting early bush fires is a common practice among the herders in Savè. Many investigations suggested that this indigenous practice enables the nutrients which are released to re-enter the vegetation and stimulate a palatable and nutritious flush growth from perennial grasses (see also Fairhead, 1991). Early fires can help to drive away mosquitoes and harmful insects and so protect the animals.

activists for its functioning. But the fact that the decision-making power
was not in the hands of the herders – some of whom were labourers who were
keeping the cattle of the people living in town – meant that this agreement
could not be maintained.

The government also intervened to resolve the many conflicts in the area.
It created an *ad hoc* commission for conflict resolution at the level of the
sous-préfecture. This commission involved the *sous-préfet*, the district officer
for rural development, the village extension worker, the police forces
(*gendarmes*), a representative of the herders and a representative of the
farmers (see also P. Onibon and Okou, 1995: 75). The role of this committee
was to mediate disputes between crop farmers and herders. However, many
herders preferred a settlement out of court when their cattle damaged a
farm, whereas many farmers preferred the resolution of conflict at the level
of the *gendarmerie*, where coercive methods are used. Consequently, many
herders did not trust this commission. The commission would have been
more effective if it had helped to generate new stakeholder organisations to
prevent and resolve conflicts at the local level. It should also have supported
existing local institutions and organisations for conflict prevention.

This case study shows that many problems, such as crop damage by the
cattle, the absence of corridor spaces and difficulty of access to watering
places, affect the herders. Serious problems occurred, like the conflicts
between herders and crop farmers. Many local initiatives emerged among
the stakeholders for resolving the above problems. However, the fact that
they lacked a decision-making capacity (*e.g.* to reorganise the area used by
the villagers and the herders) meant that there was no effective platform at
the inter-village level to overcome barriers in the rangeland resource
management, such as water, pastures, security and peace. It may be that the
absence of external intervention prevented the pooling of local initiatives.

The rangeland case study in the Savè area generated a new idea for an
additional rangeland case study. The study of the situation in Kemon led to
an exploration of the effect of external support of sustainable rangeland
development within the Chabe community.

*II.2.2   External support for developing a platform for collective rangeland
resource management in Kemon*
The second case study on rangeland issues was conducted in the village of
Kemon in the *sous-préfecture* of Ouèssè, in the northern part of the Collines.
Kemon is a Chabe village which still has a strong local organisation dealing
with the socio-economic and political dimensions of social life. The *balé* is

the local authority, the spiritual chief of the land, and the mediator of many disputes. The imam, the authority of Moslems, is also an influential authority. Many farmers in Kemon are hunters, and the *balodé*, who is the second important authority after the *balé*, is their chairman. The organisation of the hunters is strategically important. Traditionally, the hunters' role was to protect the village against aggression or attacks by other tribal groups (ethnic wars) and to protect the bush against exploitation (hunting, logging or farming) by people outside the village.

The herders have two organisations: one of the sedentary old-time herders and one for the migrant herders (*buzu*), who have different interests. The *buzu* comprise recent settlers and transmigrants, who sometimes stay for only a few days.

Serious conflicts existed between the villagers and the herders in Kemon area. Between 1983 and 1990, 28 herders and 10 farmers died in the conflicts and wars between the villagers and the *buzu*. The region became insecure for a certain period. Under these difficult circumstances, the native Chabe in many villages surrounding Kilibo decided to keep out all the *buzu* from their territory. The government also prevented the penetration of the transhumant *buzu* into the territory of Benin with the help of the army and the *gendarmerie*. The villagers of Kemon, however, adopted a different way of dealing with the transhumance problem in the Chabe community.

The local organisation of the hunters in Kemon saw the relevance of opening a debate with the herders. The *balodé* advised the villagers who felt provoked by the herders' actions on their farms not to react and return to the village. The problem would then be solved at the level of the hunters' organisation, chaired by the *balodé*. The *balodé* had his local way of approaching the problem, using the metaphor *yanpekpe* ("If you need peace, you will not touch *yanpekpe*") to explain the conditions for establishing a good relationship between the herders and the villagers. *Yanpekpe (Tragia senegalensis)* is a local plant, the mature fruit of which causes itching for a long period if it touches the human body. Thus, the metaphor suggested that, if the herders want peace while staying in the territory of Kemon, they should not create problems (not touch *yanpekpe*). The *buzu* who wanted to settle in Kemon should ensure that their cattle did not cause crop damage on the farms. The local organisation of the hunters in Kemon decided to mark the boundaries of the village and the areas where their cattle could graze, in order to avoid conflicts with the farmers. However, it was explained to the herders that the organisation would not be responsible for any problems they caused beyond the territory of Kemon.

The reasons for the villagers of Kemon to establish good relationships with the herders were economic. The *buzu* contributed to the local economy in Kemon in several ways. The herders provided the villagers with meat, milk and cheese. The butchers bought the cattle from the herders and many native Chabe in Kemon were involved in the cattle trade and made a profit from it. A hunter explained that finding wild animals was becoming harder and the herders therefore gained in importance. The *buzu* also contributed to the development of a local market. Their wives bought clothes, kitchen utensils and agricultural products. The presence of the *buzu* also created new jobs among unemployed young people in Kemon in the form of a motor taxi called *zemidjan*. They took the *buzu* from their hamlet to the village and vice-versa. Thus, transhumance had a positive socio-economic impact on the development of the local economy during this period and the village therefore welcomed the transhumants.

To sum up, the stakeholders in Kemon learned to overcome barriers to rangeland resource management. However, their initiatives were not recognised and supported by the political authorities, which preferred military intervention and sending back the migrant herders to their country. This problem may carry the risk that the local solution will not be sustained, especially since the stakeholders' perspective deviated and even contradicted the government's actions.

In contrast to Savè, the PGRN (*Projet de Gestion des Ressources Naturelles* = Project for the Management of Natural Resources) was active in the *sous-préfecture* of Ouèssè, and the local organisations in Kemon (one of the project villages) collaborated with the project to improve rangeland management. The PGRN was able to fulfil a role as mediator and negotiator, because it applied the "*appui-conseil*" (support-advice) approach instead of the coercive manner employed by the government during the Communist regime when it had fought the Fulbe transhumant herders. The support-advice framework is based on participation and the support of the stakeholders to help them sustain the actions in which they already are engaged. The principal objective of the support-advice is to provide a methodological guide for implementing various actions by villagers to improve rangeland resource management in the village of Kemon and its territory. The concrete objectives of the support-advice are:
- to establish a better social relationship between the Fulbe and the farmers;
- to effectively manage land and associated resources (vegetation and water, in particular); and

- to promote the social and economic development of the villagers and the herders.

The support-advice emphasises mediation of disputes and the development of local platforms by empowering the existing local organisation for the resolution of rangeland problems. Regular meetings between the PGRN people, who serve as mediators, and the representatives of the different parties facilitated collective decision making and the resolution of rangeland problems. This enabled concerted agreement to be reached about the payment by the herders of a tax for tree planting to avoid degradation of grazing areas. Another success was the building of a wider local platform in the form of a tripartite committee for collective rangeland management, consisting of representatives of the hunters' organisation, old-time herders and transmigrants.

The idea of *responsabilisation*, the transfer of certain competencies (roles, negotiation, mediation and conflict resolution) was used for sustaining negotiated agreements among the villagers in Kemon and the different categories of Fulbe. Among the tasks that were perceived to be the responsibility of the stakeholders' organisation under the support-advice framework were participation in the delimitation of grazing areas, collecting taxes from the *buzu* using the grazing area, managing the funds that result from tax collection, and resolving conflicts between Fulbe and farmers. The stakeholders and the PGRN jointly perceived these roles. They were transferred through training (*e.g.* in the analysis of maps and aerial photographs, keeping documents for land registration and the management of funds collected from taxes) and non-formal education of people.

However, in the absence of effective decentralisation of power to the stakeholders, there was no enabling policy framework for generating collective agency in the local setting, such as decision-making capacity and statutory power. This problem presents some of the risks of failure in sustaining the institutions and organisations which were jointly generated by the stakeholders in Kemon and the PGRN intervention. A solution to this problem was found by transforming the local organisation of hunters in Kemon and the *Brigades Locales de Transhumance* into an NGO. The COGEF (*Comité de Gestion du Foncier Pastoral* = Committee for the management of pastoral tenure) was created.

II.2.3 Comparative analysis and conclusion
Both of the situations studied in the Chabe community revealed that rangeland resource management problems are not only a question of carrying capacity, 33

as is often claimed. Some barriers, such as lack of concerted action between the Fulbe and villagers, serious conflicts and wars, and the absence of organisations and institutions for rangeland resource management, are more critical. These issues affected the failure of rangeland resource management.

In Kemon, the development of collective decision-making capacity made possible successful collective action to overcome barriers in rangeland resource management. Local stakeholders realised their mutual interdependence and developed a negotiated agreement and concerted action. Platform development was successful with external support and created the condition for decision making, monitoring, sanctions and exclusions. This joint learning generated social capital for continuing action if the political context provides an enabling environment.

In Savè, the stakeholders who were engaged in collective learning lacked decision-making power. Different interest groups did not realise their mutual interdependence as they did in Kemon. They did not meet and negotiate agreement or take concerted action. Many failures can be explained at this level.

Barriers to the sustainable management of rangeland resources can be overcome if the different stakeholders adopt collective action, develop platforms for decision making, monitoring, sanctions and exclusions, at the level of many *gaa*, villages and regions.

II.3 Watershed development with indigenous peoples in two eco-zones of Benin

A watershed is an area drained by a single watercourse system (White and Runge, 1994). Watersheds involve multiple and interconnected natural resources such as soil, water and vegetation (forests) and are ecologically fragile. Land areas in watersheds – for which the PGRN used the term *bassins versants* – are sensitive to soil erosion when not covered with vegetation. Watershed development has become a worldwide agricultural development problem, especially in developing countries (*e.g.* Doolette and William, 1990; Ninan, 1998). Many watershed development initiatives aim at improving the productivity and production potential of the ecologically fragile and disadvantaged farming areas through the adoption of soil and water conservation techniques. Others, however, position the watershed development issue at the level of community mobilisation (*cf.* Tiffen and Mortimore, 1992).

This study explored the conditions for successful watershed management with local people by comparing two situations in Benin. One situation was studied on the Adja plateau in the province of Couffo. The other was located in the *sous-préfecture* of Ouèssè in the Collines province. Both locations suffer from soil erosion problems which cause the degradation of agricultural lands. The PGRN project is being implemented to support village communities to sustainably manage watershed resources and to help them overcome serious erosion problems which cause the degradation of agricultural fields.

"Scaling up" is the core issue for watershed development in both sub-cases. Within the boundary established in the intervention areas in Couffo and Collines there are many villages, and in each village many households are cultivating watershed areas. The physical properties of watersheds mean that downstream stakeholders need the cooperation of upstream stakeholders if watershed development is to be successful. Watershed development necessarily involves coordination between individual stakeholders. Scaling up watershed development efforts from individual cultivation parcels to the whole watershed area identified for improvement is essential. This process requires successful collective action among individuals, groups of stakeholders or villages in the intervention areas. It also requires a structural process for developing platforms of stakeholders to enable collective decisions to be made at the level of the whole watershed. A concrete example of the importance of such platforms is where collective decision making, negotiation and conflict resolution are needed to establish well-defined rights and duties for land-holding.

II.3.1   Scaling up watershed development with the Adja people

The Adja region is one of the most densely populated in Benin. The population density is 240-400 inhabitants per km². The farmers in this region practise a kind of intensive cultivation in which they combine inter-cropping, relay-cropping and indigenous agro-forestry based on oil palm trees. The farmers use the rotation of crops with oil palm and diversification of varieties as means of intensification. The Adja farmers practise minimal tillage. Weeds and crop refuse are left on the soil surface. In the Adja region, the watershed problems consist of water erosion, decline of soil fertility, inundation of downstream areas and degradation of relic forests on hills in the upstream areas of watersheds.

According to the PGRN and the donors, the main problems in the Adja region are the stagnation of agricultural production, the mounting pressure on land and decreasing productive capacity of the agro-forest-pastoral ecosystems within the watersheds. The Adja farmers' cultivation practices are therefore seen as the main cause of land degradation in the watersheds. The promotion of soil and water conservation techniques (*e.g.* gullies, contour planting of *vetiver* grasses) and tree planting are seen as the most important goals of intervention. Such an approach inevitably leads to the neglect of

35

some important aspects, such as the institutions and organisations required for sustaining these technical measures.

The runoff problem is well perceived by Adja farmers and several expressions are used to describe it, for instance, *eshi lo gbo* (the water floods the crops in the farm) and *eshi djanonta non gnigban* (the water "cuts" the head of the soil). This means that, according to the Adja farmers, runoff has two negative effects: it destroys the crops and carries the arable soil away. Adja people had experimented with several solutions, and adopted a sophisticated oil palm-based farming system as an answer to declining soil fertility. They do not ridge, however, although contour farming – the most efficient way for controlling soil erosion in the PGRN technological package – requires ridging. A critical issue for watershed development in Couffo is therefore whether the Adja farmers can change their way of cultivation from minimal tillage to ridging. Stakeholder analysis had revealed that the majority of the Adja farmers have access to land under indirect rules. This may not motivate them to invest in using new techniques for watershed development.

This case study afforded opportunities for exploring various dimensions of facilitation by the watershed managers of the PGRN project. Intervention started when an individual, group or village made a request for support. Once a request is made, agreement forums are organised in order to arrive at a shared perception of the problems. In the first agreement forum, the stakeholders present their problems and the need for their resolution. Then, meetings are planned for discussing specific problems, such as combating soil erosion, afforestation or the construction of infrastructure. The discussion at each meeting is about the relevance of the problem at stake, solutions already tried without success and the contribution (in terms of labour, money, etc.) of stakeholders to the costs of resolving the problem. The purpose of these discussions is to arrive at decisions about the outline of the process. This includes the organisation required (the formation of stakeholders' committees), the structuring of the process and the training needs. In the Adja region, this strategy made possible the implementation of some concrete actions by the PGRN team.

An immediate effect of the initial forums was that they facilitated the development of a partnership relationship between some stakeholders and the PGRN team. The nature of activities for solving the problems covered many issues at different levels. Tree planting and animal raising, for instance, were individually requested. Financial assistance for the processing of agricultural products was requested by groups of women. Activities like the protection of villages' mud houses against runoff, the improvement of drinking water sources and road construction, were requested at the village level. Many of the activities requested by the stakeholders are close to the objective of PGRN intervention, such as the protection of the houses in the villages against runoff, tree planting in individual plots, reducing the damage caused by runoff on the farms and improving the fertility of the soil. Dealing with the stakeholders' priorities gave the PGRN team the opportunity to learn how the stakeholders could develop a common appreciation of watershed development problems.

An example of an interaction between the PGRN team and the stakeholders, in which the PGRN learned to live with indigenous knowledge, concerned the issue of ridging. The Adja farmers in the village Dekpo (in Aplahoué) did not practise ridging for cultivation. The contour farming technique in the technological package of the PGRN did not make sense to them. Living with the Adja farmers' knowledge was the only way for the professionals to initiate watershed development in Aplahoué. The PGRN team organised a forum to identify the appropriate watershed development techniques through interactive processes.

Firstly, contour ridging was explained to the farmers, but they found it difficult because they practise minimum tillage for cultivation. The second proposal comprised planting nitrogen-fixing shrubs (*Acacia auriculifiormis*; *Gliciridia sepium*) as hedgerows along the contour lines, leaving the strips between the hedgerows for cultivation. The third option proposed to the farmers was to construct ridges of stones (*cordon pierreux*), following the contour lines. The Adja farmers chose the second option, the hedgerows between crops, because the collection of stones might be too time-consuming.

The PGRN provided subsidies and incentives for soil erosion control and training on how to cultivate along contour lines. Training was offered also in the establishment of cottage industries and on health problems. PGRN used various communication strategies (*animation rurale*) to stimulate voluntary behavioural change in the short term, such as folk media (especially local singers and folklore groups) and mass media (radio).

As the request for intervention or support covered several development activities (infrastructure, income-generating activities, and resource management) which called for competence beyond that of the PGRN, network management became a crucial activity for the watershed managers in Couffo. The project therefore manages a network in which an expertise bureau, governmental and non-governmental organisations and credit opportunities for women also form a part.

One of the efforts undertaken by the stakeholders was the construction of a system of trenches in a village which had suffered from frequent inundation during the rainy season. In the past, the villagers had waited for the government to come and solve the problem. The PGRN explained that they could help with tools and a surveyor, but the people would have to organise themselves and do the work. A local committee was formed, in which the younger people played the main role in organising the men to participate during a number of days in the digging of trenches. The formal village chief "inspected" the work and was given the honour due to him. Hundreds of metres of trenches were dug but, no less important, the self assurance of the villagers grew and they started to think about a similar mobilisation of manpower to build an all-weather road and to use the runoff water for a constructive purpose like rice or fish growing.

Successful collective action was effective in situations where the stakeholders perceived their interdependence, as in the case of erosion control. Runoff had a collective negative effect (the destruction of mud houses) for all the villagers. Nevertheless, despite the incentive policy adopted by the PGRN, the *animation rurale* processes, and existing institutional frameworks, the scaling up of watershed development from the farms of individual participating stakeholders to the whole watershed area, has so far not been effective. The patterns of individual farm layouts in the watershed under siege did not correspond to a specific village land-use area. There is no village *terroir* in the Adja region. The stakeholders in various micro-watersheds do not live in the same villages as those where *Comités de Gestion de Terroir* are in operation, yet platforms for pooling a systematic treatment of micro-watersheds towards a watershed development based on inter-village cooperation has not emerged in Couffo.

II.3.2   Scaling up watershed development with the Mahi people
The Mahi people are the dominant ethnic group in Ouèssè. Their main activity is agriculture and, in contrast to the Adja farmers in Couffo, they practise shifting cultivation. They do not use fertilisers in the shifting cultivation areas. Consequently, the agro-ecological environment has degraded through continuous land clearing. The PGRN and the donor (the *Agence Française de Développement*) perceived the cultivation methods of the Mahi farmers as the main problem. The critical issue for watershed development is that they should be able to clear more land for shifting cultivation on the old fallow, which contains areas of fertile soil. Watershed development, however, demands a radical change. Can the Mahi farmers invest in an agricultural

parcel for the sake of watershed development and abandon their shifting cultivation on the old fallow? This question is critical, because the expected yield after using new watershed development techniques is lower than the yield on the old fallow, where the Mahi farmers do not use fertilisers.

The NGO known as GERAM (*Groupe d'expertise et d'ingenierie rurales pour l'auto-promotion du monde paysan*), which was contracted to implement the PGRN, followed a similar process to that of the PGRN in Couffo to achieve a common appreciation of the problems. As in Couffo, the PGRN and the stakeholders had different perceptions. The watershed problems perceived by the Mahi farmers were based on indicators and direct observations, such as the drying up of the water in wells and rivers, increasing scarcity of firewood, land degradation on the farms caused by runoff and the long distance from fertile agricultural plots. According to the same farmers, however, other problems which affect their livelihood are equally or more urgent. These concern labour availability, drinking water, infrastructure and the problem of transporting their crops after harvest (maize, cassava, groundnuts, and cotton). The women preferred financial assistance for the processing of agricultural products which would provide an important source of income. The migrant farmers – who are not allowed to plant trees on their parcels[8] – consider land tenure security to be crucial.

Because of the opportunity Mahi farmers had to shift their plots on the old fallow, they did not perceive the watershed development problems as a priority. Under these circumstances, external support for scaling up watershed development first required the stakeholders in different villages to reach a common appreciation of the problems, adopt collective action and develop platforms for decision making.

Table 2 Quantification of the nature of the support requested by the stakeholders in Ouèssè

Domain of activities	Nature of the demands made by the stakeholders in %			Total
	Individual level	Group level	Village level	
Natural resource management activities	23 (40%)	32 (37%)	16 (28%)	71 (36%)
Income-generating activities	20 (34%)	51 (59%)	1 (2%)	72 (36%)
Infrastructure	10 (17%)	4 (4%)	29 (52%)	43 (21%)
Social and cultural activities	5 (9%)	-	10 (18%)	15 (7%)
Total	58 (100%)	87 (100%)	56 (100%)	201 (100%)

Source: Annual report of the GERAM team (see Adjinacou, Aho and Agbo, 1995).

---

8   Planting trees in Mahi society is a kind of land appropriation.

The problem identification process stimulated many requests for assistance. Support was requested for:
- natural resource management (*e.g.* protection of the houses in the villages, tree planting and reduction of damage caused by runoff on the farms);
- income-generating activities (*e.g.* bee keeping in gallery forest, gardening and horticulture by the women's groups and livestock raising (pigs, chickens);
- the construction of infrastructure (a well, bridge, road and a house for storing inputs); and
- social and cultural activities (*e.g.* radio programmes).

Table 2 shows that livelihood strategies were considered more important than watershed development. GERAM adopted the strategy of focussing on the stakeholders' needs as a starting point for intervention. In this way, trust could be built up for arriving at the core issue of watershed development. The idea was to work closely with the stakeholders on various issues, in the course of which they would discover the importance of using techniques for watershed control.

The activities of the GERAM for solving the erosion problem started with the creation of functional committees, which can be perceived as different platforms for implementing various activities at the village or group level. Examples of such activities were periodical discussion of the progress of the activities, and organising and following up activities such as afforestation and bee keeping. Existing local organisations such as the Village Development Committee (*Comité de Développement du Village*) and the Village Consultative Council (*Conseil Consultatif du Village*) were also used.

The incentives and *animation rurale* provided by he GERAM could be considered successful. Horizontal diffusion (replication) of contour farming as a means of erosion control was high. A particular problem arose, however, from the introduction of *vetiver* grasses in contour cultivation. Many farmers adopted this technique and planted *vetiver* grass and cashew trees on the main contour lines. However, the introduction of *vetiver* created new problems: stakeholders did not have time to prune the *vetiver*, which shelters rats and snakes. The rats destroy the maize stored on the farms and the snakes kill the chickens. Some farmers suggested replacing *vetiver* by *Cajanus cajan*, another leguminous shrub, and others suggested growing pineapples. Farmers knew Cajanus as a source of edible peas and suggested using it in order to obtain a double effect. This raised a debate among PGRN experts about the efficacy of the farmers' suggestions. The experts feared that the weaker root system of Cajanus might not be strong enough to prevent erosion. At the time of writing, this question had not yet been tested experimentally.

Another problem was that of coordination between the different organisations. Unlike the situation in the Couffo case study, existing local organisations in the *sous-préfecture* of Ouèssè already operated at the level of the whole Mahi community. Although this condition might be favourable for scaling up watershed development, the decentralisation of certain powers (*e.g.* statutory power) from the government administrative bodies to the local people was still not effective. The policy context in the communities in Ouèssè did not yet allow for collective action in watershed development.

During a periodical meeting between the GERAM team and watershed development committees from different Mahi villages in Ouèssè, participating farmers realised the importance of creating a higher level organisation (*cf.* Adjinacou *et al.*, 1995). They perceived that isolated action by small groups in different villages would not realise the potential importance of these activities. They used the metaphor SEDOKU (*Our common wealth from nature*) to qualify the natural resources. They then expressed the need to have a structure for concerted action (*cadre de concertation*) to manage these resources. After this meeting, the GERAM team initiated a scaling-up process for watershed development.

The inter-village organisation that needed to be created was called SEDOKU and UIGREN (*Union Inter-villageoise pour la Gestion des Ressources Naturelles* = Inter-village Union for Natural Resource Management). It was intended to be a local negotiating body and a higher decision-making entity for covenants, new norms and regulations for collective natural resource management. It would also take an active part in the identification and monitoring and control of concrete resource management projects for the region.

II.3.3 Comparative analysis and conclusions

The present case study of watershed development problems was perceived at the policy level. However, the two situations studied showed that a joint learning path, involving the intervening party and the stakeholders, makes possible a move towards a common appreciation of these problems.

Existing cultural practices have some implications for the way the solutions and innovations in watershed development should be approached. For instance, the Adja farmers' method of farming imposed interactive learning for identifying appropriate erosion control techniques.

In both the Adja and Mahi regions, institutional frameworks and policy contexts appeared to be crucial issues for watershed development. A concrete

41

example was the absence of a consistent property right institution, which created a barrier for many stakeholders.

The most critical question which emerges from the present case study is why the scaling-up process started successfully in the Collines (*sous-préfecture* of Ouèssè) and not in Couffo. In Ouèssè, existing organisations at the level of the Mahi region (*e.g.* functional committees for watershed development and the King of Ouèssè) were already active and they were a driving force for the scaling-up process. Nevertheless, the initiative of the GERAM team in enabling operational committees from different villages to meet and discuss was a determinant factor for the collective perception of interdependence for resource management (the SEDOKU metaphor). This condition also triggered the process of scaling-up and the creation of a higher platform, such as the UIGREN/SEDOKU, thus creating a condition for sustainable resource management at the level of the whole watershed. Such a situation had not yet been realised in the Adja region, because of the failure to start the generation of organisations at a higher level of social aggregation.

II.4 Collective action and resource-flow management for improving soil fertility by a women's group in Djeffa, Benin

This section deals with the initiative of a women's group in Djeffa, which developed several activities to improve soil stability and fertility for horticultural development. This case study assumed that the division of labour between women and men, and gender-sensitive knowledge and responsibilities are relevant to resource management.

With more than 240 inhabitants per km², Djeffa is a densely populated coastal village in the southern part of the Ouémé Province in Benin. The village has a population of 4,264 inhabitants (INSAE, 1993), with the Xla people as the dominant ethnic group. As in all coastal regions in Benin, the dominant natural vegetation in Djeffa is the coconut tree (*Cocos nucifera*). The soils of the Djeffa area are very sandy, poor in organic matter and have a low water-holding capacity (Schelhaas, 1978: 22). The poor soil fertility is a serious constraint on agriculture. Crops do not grow well on the sandy soils if the latter are not treated with organic matter to improve their stability and fertility. The climatic conditions are comparable with those in the Adja region.

Socio-economic activities in the village are varied. There is a dynamic small-scale trade in such products as sugar, soap, fish, maize, *gari*[9] and coconut oil. The many swampy areas in Djeffa, which are inundated during the rainy season, are used for sugar cane cultivation. The local people grow vegetables

---

42   [9]   Gari is a product obtained from processing cassava.

during the two dry seasons and tomato, maize and cassava during the rainy season.

Landownership in Djeffa is highly diverse. Some rich people from urban areas (*e.g.* Cotonou and Porto-Novo) have bought land in the Djeffa area for the planting of coconut trees. For the people in Djeffa, borrowing, sharecropping, and renting are the most common ways of gaining access to land for agricultural and horticultural activities. Food insecurity is a problem and the children are often undernourished.

Against this background, seven women found a way of coping with their situation. They had started a *tontine*, a rotational savings fund, which enabled them to invest in commercial activities and the processing of agricultural products. On advice of a man who had returned from Nigeria, where he had seen women's cooperatives, the women decided to broaden their activity and set up a production cooperative. They developed an integrated system of activities which help to produce organic matter which can be used to improve the stability and fertility of their soil for horticulture.

II.4.1   The principle of resource-flow management in Djeffa
The principle of resource-flow management as applied by the women in Djeffa is based on three basic interrelated economic activities: coconut-fruit processing, pig raising and horticulture. The by-products of these activities are used to improve the stability and fertility of the soil.

The first activity of the women's group is the processing of coconuts. They first separate the kernel from the husk. The latter is used as firewood and the kernels are used for the production of coconut oil, for which purpose they are first crushed in a mill. Then, water is added to the pasty substance obtained from the milling. This mixture is filtered, separating the bran from the liquid, that is boiled to obtain the oil. The bran of the kernel (called *dja* by the women) is used for the second activity, pig raising.

Feeding is an important constraint on pig raising in Djeffa. Increasing the scale of kernel processing into oil can provide more *dja*, which is used as pig food. Thus, a strong link has developed between the first and the second activity. The pigs are raised on a bedding which consists of grasses, which are specially collected for this purpose. The mixture of the pig's dung, urine and the bedding ferments to produce a considerable quantity of organic matter.

The women were aware of the need to add nutrients to the soil to increase the yield of plants. The manure obtained from pig raising enabled them to develop horticultural activities and produce vegetables (fontete, gboma, eggplants and tomatoes) without using chemical fertilisers.

II.4.2 Collective action and resource-flow management by the women's
group before the democratisation area
A crucial problem at the beginning of the women's initiative was the lack of
funds to buy a large quantity of coconuts for processing. This processing
was necessary to increase the scale of pig raising and obtain a sufficient
quantity of organic matter for horticulture. Other problems the women
experienced were leadership (too many members wanted to lead the group),
equal participation and the absence of immediate profit, which caused some
members to leave.

Ensuring the provision of labour was the most difficult. Labour was
needed for the construction of the pigsties, the daily feeding of the pigs and
the collection of grass for bedding. On the horticultural side, labour was
needed for the preparation of the nurseries and seedbeds, the collection of
compost from the pigsty, transplanting and daily watering, harvesting and
selling. Many members of the group were unwilling to contribute much effort
to these activities.

A strategic decision in solving the labour problem was to include men
in the group. Some activities did not fit the local cultural perception of the
gender division of labour. Accepting male members allowed the women to
leave such tasks as the construction of pigsties and preparing the seedbeds
to men. Instead of using wage labour for the tasks the women were not able
to do, a solution was to accept men as members of the group.

Moreover, women started monitoring the participation in collective
activities. Sanctions were introduced to deal with free riders. The fact that
many women and men were excluded could be a sign that these sanctions
were effective and provided an environment in which the members had the
assurance that everybody followed the rules. Together with decision-making
arrangements and coordination at group level, the measures to stimulate
more participation were important and helped to maintain the group and
generate successful collective action.

But external support also contributed to the dynamics for ongoing
resource-flow management activities. At the time the women's group emerged,
the policy context was characterised by a monopoly of governmental
organisations in supporting local organisations. Under the Communist
regime, CARDER was the only extension organisation. It restricted itself to
conventional agricultural extension in a top-down approach and could not
provide the women's group with sufficient opportunities to satisfy their
various needs and support the activities in which they were already engaged.
The women's group benefited, however, from an NGO created in 1984, the
CIRAPIP (*Centre de d'Information et de Recherches pour l' Auto-Promotion*

à l'Initiative Paysanne = the Information and Research Centre for the Auto-Promotion of Peasant Initiatives). This NGO established contact with the women when the group was created. It carried out a literacy programme in order to help the stakeholders to take responsibility, to increase their accountability and to ensure the proper functioning of the group. They also introduced a much-appreciated social assistance programme. But the most important issue in the support of the CIRAPIP was providing the members with food through negotiation with the EC representation in Benin. They received maize, rice, oil and milk for collective activities. This opportunity motivated the members and they appreciated the extent to which the maintenance of the group benefited.

II.4.3 Collective action and resource-flow management by the women's group during the democratisation area

At the end of 1989, the failure of the Marxist regime in the face of a severe economic crisis in Benin led to a shift in the national political system. Benin adopted a liberal regime and a multiparty system in the Conférence Nationale. These changes created a new dynamic and opportunities in local rural development. The monopoly of CARDER in rural development activities changed: associations were allowed and a mechanism was created for their official recognition. The new political environment made possible the emergence of many NGOs for the promotion of rural development.

Within this new context, the women's group in Djeffa started looking for opportunities to enhance their resource-flow management activities. In 1991, the group joined a networking movement for the development of sustainable agriculture in Benin. In January 1992 the group became a founding member of a network called REDAD (Réseau de Développement d'Agriculture Durable = Network for the Development of Sustainable Agriculture). This network aims at promoting sustainable agriculture in Benin with local organisations such as the women's group in Djeffa.

The women's group benefited from many REDAD activities. Joint field visits organised by REDAD stimulated the exchange of experiences and generated collective learning among the participants. They thus discovered how mucuna (Mucuna pruriens var. utilis) is used to improve the fertility of the soil and to control a tough weed (Imperata cylindrica). Alley-cropping systems using Gliricidia sepium and Acacia auriculiformis were also learned. The group participated in a field discussion at the Sê agro-pastoral centre (in Mono province), where they learned how goat and sheep production can be linked to biodynamic horticulture. The women also received formal training, e.g. in the identification and implementation of integrated activities, compost-making techniques and leadership.

The NGOs had a great interest in local organisations such as the women's group in Djeffa, which already had some successful initiatives. The group's experience with resource-flow management was, for instance, a model at the beginning of the REDAD. Paralleling this network movement, the group multiplied their contacts with many NGOs, which is a sign of its dynamic.

One of the NGOs, CEBEDES (*Centre Béninois pour le Développement Economique et Social*) introduced a new form of credit for the women's group to strengthen its *tontine* activity. A 200,000 CFA (US$ 286) loan with an interest rate of 1% rotated among the members of the group. Depending on the savings of a member, he or she could request a loan from the CEBEDES fund for individual activities, *e.g.* to start a personal business.

CIRAPIP involved the women's group in the governmental PILSA (*Projet d'Intervention Locale pour la Sécurité Alimentaire*) project on food security. The support of PILSA/CIRAPIP made possible the construction of a storage house for maize selling.

The involvement of the women's group in a large network created many opportunities and reduced the incentives for members to leave the group. These dynamics have stimulated the local CARDER agent in Djeffa to change his practices. He decided to help the women's group in their new approach and to work for their specific interests.

II.4.4   Conclusions

The present case study demonstrates that resource-flow management can be effective for improving soil fertility in Djeffa if successful collective action can be maintained. The factors that affect successful collective action are related to the nature of the group itself, the context and the existing opportunities.

As far as the group is concerned, the capacity for generating institutions such as collective decision making, monitoring, and sanctioning appeared to be critical factors for maintaining successful collective action.

With respect to the context, the case study revealed that a shift in the political system of the country made grass-roots development processes more dynamic. The more the context makes possible the development of pluriform initiatives (*e.g.* the emergence of NGOs in Benin), the greater is the access to external support. In this way, new opportunities and conditions are created for continuing ecological practices such as resource-flow management, which require successful collective action.

II.5 Regenerating the Maro Forest in Burkina Faso: the development of platforms for resource management

II.5.1 Antecedents

The Maro Forest – named after one of the 21 villages in the area – is located in the south-western province of Tuy (formerly Houet) in Burkina Faso. The forest is situated along the Bobo-Dioulasso – Dédougou road about 75 km northwest of Bobo-Dioulasso. It covers an area of about 56,227 ha and has a population of more than 40,000. At village level, the population can be divided into migrants, cattle breeders and natives.

The main economic activities in the area are farming – with maize, sorghum and cotton as the main crops – and cattle breeding. According to a census taken in 1992, there were 13,770 animals herded in the forest, of which 9,613 were cows, donkeys and horses and 4,157 were sheep and goats. Other activities are apiculture and crafts. Each village has some holy places in the forest, where sacrifices to the gods are made and no human being has the right to use these places in other ways.

Until the colonisation period, forests were common goods. The ownership and decision-making power were in the hands of large native families, who divided rights among the local population. At that time, the community had the power to refuse access to outsiders, prevent encroachment by its own members and establish restrictions on cutting trees. Under French rule, especially from the 1930s to the 1950s, many forests were made a public property resource. The forests were "classified", which meant that the local population could only collect nuts, fruits, medicinal plants and dead branches. Tree cutting and cultivation in the forest area were forbidden. Since the forest became state-owned, the population no longer felt responsible for it. Illegal woodcutting and cultivation occurred. The state, through the Forest Agency, was unable to enforce its policy of forest protection and prevention of misuse. Thus, a "tragedy of the commons" was created. The state aimed to combat deforestation and forest degradation, but did not have sufficient means to control and manage its property.

After independence, solutions were sought to prevent further forest degradation. With the aim of providing the rural population with sufficient fuel wood, ensuring the provision of fuel wood to urban centres and improving the productivity of the natural forest, parts of the natural forests were replaced with industrial plantations. Exotic (*Eucalyptus* and *Gmelina*) as well as native (*e.g. Khaya senegalensis*, *Anogeissus lerocarpus* and *Tamarindus indica*) species were planted. *Eucalyptus* is used mainly for the production of fuel wood and timber, while *Gmelina* is used mainly for timber.

The plantation was an industrial one and the population received 1,000 CFA (US$ 1.40) for a day's work in it. Because of the plantation's industrial character, the local population did not regard it as their property. With regard to the natural forest, nothing had changed and the population continued to treat it as an open access resource. It was soon realised that the creation of industrial plantations, based on the destruction of natural vegetation, was not the desired solution.

II.5.2   Management of the Maro Forest under the PNGT

During the last few years, decentralisation and local participation have been introduced and private ownership is allowed. Decentralisation provides for the handing over of certain competencies to local communities. The forests remain state-owned, but can be contracted for management to individuals or groups, in return for their agreement to chop wood only at certain times and at certain places. *Groupements de Gestion Forestière* (GGFs) were created for the management of the plantation and the sale of the timber. These groups are expected to maintain the plantations in good condition by replanting, cleaning the firebreaks and guarding the wood. The population working in the plantation under this more participatory approach regarded it as their private property, which had to be well managed.

By using a *gestion des terroirs* approach, the government tried to make people aware of the need to curb the degradation of natural resources and to manage the Maro Forest sustainably. It also promoted – through the creation of the GGFs – the development of a local basis for solving common problems in land-use management. The government did not, however, surrender its official ownership. It aimed to achieve co-management between the state and the local population in the use of the forest. This means that the state remained the official owner of the forest, but that the population has the use rights. These rights are, however, restricted by state rules. Thus, the forest was given a *de facto* status between a common property good, which allows the resource to be used by defined groups of villagers, and public (= government) property. The population recognises this mixed status, considers the plantations in the forest to be theirs and is willing to invest in managed afforestation. The (officially protected) natural forest, however, is still considered to be an open access property, in which people chop trees illegally. The major problem until 1993 was the pressure of farmers and herdsmen on the classified forest. To solve this problem, the PNGT tried to explain to the local population why they should leave the forest, created the GGFs, and arranged for the exploitation and commercialisation of wood from the plantations. At that time, all the plots in the Maro Forest were cultivated with cotton, which is a major threat to all forests. Within a few years, the PNGT had persuaded the 665 farmers who still cultivated in the forest to leave, so that it was no longer used for cultivation. Fourteen GGFs had been created and a lot of wood was sold (UGF, 1995).

The specific aims of the co-management of forest resources were:
- to improve and manage the forest resources in a sustainable way;
- to contribute to the resolution of farmer-herdsmen conflicts;
- to make communities aware of the way the forest should be protected and exploited;
- to maintain biodiversity; and
- to conserve historical and cultural places (EMP, 1996).

After informing the local administration, partner agencies and village authorities of the project and asking for their cooperation, the co-management process started with a 5-day participatory diagnosis with the community. Several tools were used for this diagnosis, such as maps, photos, Venn diagrams[10] and seasonal calendars. The participatory diagnosis stimulated the local population to think about their problems, and led to a search for collective solutions. In this learning process, both PNGT members and direct local stakeholders learned about the situation and the possible solutions. This participatory diagnosis can be seen as a temporal platform, but it is not always certain that all the stakeholders took part. The non-integration of herdsmen and, to a lesser degree, migrants into the community might well have led to the under-representation of these groups in the diagnosis, even if they theoretically had an equal chance to participate in taking decisions on how to undertake collective action.

It was during the participatory diagnosis that the local population agreed to change the property regime of the forest from a public to a more common one. Firstly, everybody who still cultivated in the forest had to leave. The PNGT tried to make people aware of why they needed to leave the forest plots, but although people said that they understood the motives, they in fact left by threat of force.[11]

To compensate for this loss of plots, the PNGT proposed giving local people the management of the plantation, which was formerly owned by a project. The PNGT also proposed facilitating their relations with the state agencies which control the commercialisation of plantation timber. The local population was convinced that the plantation would provide them with

---

10 Venn diagrams are pictures – usually of overlapping circles – which visualise relationships and interactions between individuals, groups or variables.

11 The PNGT warned that the forest agents would evict people who did not leave the forest voluntarily.

revenues and they accepted. The negotiation thus resulted in co-management between the local population and the state.

After the participatory diagnosis, a local platform for decision making was created, the GGF. This platform manages and controls the cutting of wood in the plantation. The wood is now cut according to a plan drawn up by the PNGT. Every member of the GGF is allowed to participate in the exploitation of the "common good". By entering the GGF, the new member accepts the rules about "taking less" and "giving more". Before signing up in the GGF, the member has to participate in cleaning the firebreaks.

Several GGFs together form an association. The aim was to give this association responsibility for the management of the natural forest, but this does not seem to work. The associations remained theoretical constructs of the PNGT, without a clear function. There still is a need for a federation of associations or a platform at the inter-territory level for the management of the entire forest.

The strength of the local platforms for co-management between the state and the local population is that they give individuals the possibility of benefiting by earning money from woodcutting in the dry season, during which no other income-generating activities are available. The GGF also spreads decision-making power across several members of the family (men and women) in contrast to the monopolist position of the family head in the case of cotton. In this way, an important condition for successful collective action is met, i.e. that the local people should reap significant benefits from changes in local resource use.

Another strength of the co-management process is that rules to prevent, sanction and monitor free riding are successfully implemented. Participation in the cleaning of firebreaks is a prerequisite for participation in woodcutting. When people do not help in cleaning the firebreaks, they have to pay an amount for each workday. Since this payment is disproportionately high, people respect the cleaning rule. Consequently, free riding by woodcutters without helping to maintain the forest is out of the question.

Another strong point is that watches are organised so that wood which is placed at the roadsides cannot be stolen. Everybody has his turn in preventing such theft and is willing to participate, because it may be his own wood that is stolen.

Finally, a mechanism for conflict resolution has been created in the form of an assembly which will judge and eventually punish the culprits. Such a system already existed for violating traditional rules (for example, with respect to holy rivers and trees), but it was adapted to the implementation of new rules.

The process also showed some weaknesses. Firstly, not all the local people benefit from the new arrangement of earning money from the selling of wood. This way of earning money does not fit into the cultural pattern of herdsmen and they refuse to collaborate. In the Fulbe culture, it is a shame to earn money through "slave work" and this is exactly how the Fulbe herdsmen perceive the cutting of wood. In contrast to farmers, who were compensated for leaving the forest with the selling of wood, herdsmen gained no advantage to compensate for the loss of access to the forest.

A second weakness is the lack of vested tenure rights for migrants. They therefore participate in woodcutting only to earn some money, but are not motivated to invest in long-term management of a territory which is not theirs. This adversely affects the operation of the GGF.

Thirdly, the PNGT has taken on the role of an intermediary rather than as facilitator. As a consequence, there is no direct communication between the local population and the traders. Direct contact between different stakeholders might lead to a better understanding of ecological processes and sustainable forest management and therefore to better collaboration between the different groups.

A fourth weakness in the co-management is that the importance and role of platforms is not recognised. This is particularly the case with the trader organisations (i.e. the organisation of donkey cart holders (GEBC) and the organisation of lorry drivers (GETBC). The Forest Agency communicates directly with the traders, but not with these organisations. Consequently, these organisations have lost their power and, with it, their control over illegal sales. This means that an essential control and power system has been destroyed, which could be solved through renewed communication between the Forest Agency and the two trader organisations.

A weakness of the conflict resolution mechanism is that it is influenced by cultural rules. This meant, in the case of one of the villages, that a corrupt village elder could not be punished. Relations of trust and reciprocity seem to be lacking when migrants and natives work together.

Another weak point is vulnerability to corruption. This applies to the commercialisation process, which is entirely controlled by the state, and to the sanctioning mechanisms at the village level, which are held by the forest agents. Corruption, together with organisational problems, poor leadership and lack of trust between the members cause members to abandon their faith in their organisations.

A final weakness is directly related to the use of the natural forest. Because the natural forest is exploited illegally, the traders are confronted with unfair competition from natural timber – which consumers prefer to the species from plantations – which is offered on the market. Sustainable management of the natural forest is indispensable for achieving a more sustainable management of the plantations. Where the state itself is not capable of controlling illegal activities, a solution may lie in transferring this power to local organisations (GGF, GEBC, GTEBC) and providing them with an effective sanction and monitoring system.

II.5.3   Concluding remarks

The Maro Forest is rapidly being deforested and, like the other forests in Burkina Faso, faces a web of social dilemmas. People exploit the forest in their own interest without taking account of the collective interest. Even if people do not farm any more, animals enter and people illegally cut wood. People should agree not to enter and not to chop more wood than can be sustained. This is often indicated by the metaphor "take less". People should also invest in forest management, for example, by replanting and monitoring illegal users. This can be expressed by the metaphor "give more". The problem of common goods dilemmas can be overcome when stakeholders agree on "taking less" (*i.e.* cutting less wood) through collective action. This requires some control to be exercised over public goods, *e.g.* through monitoring, sanctions, etc. Without these collective actions, natural resource management is not possible. For successful collective action, overcoming the public goods dilemma is also important. Stakeholders should be ready to "give more".

The joint learning process, which led from centralisation to collective action, is still continuing. Platforms on which all stakeholders meet, negotiate and come to common decisions have to be improved, for example, by strengthening the organisations that represent the different interests. Building up trust and providing clear legal securities are necessary for that process to succeed.

II.6   Developing platforms for the management of a forest-pastoral zone in the Houet Province, Burkina-Faso

II.6.1   Gestion des terroirs: concepts, stakeholders, problems and perceptions

The present case study deals with problems in implementing the *gestion des terroirs* approach by the *Programme National de Gestion des Terroirs* (PNGT) in the Houet province of Burkina Faso. In this specific context, *gestion des terroirs* is defined as a rural development approach based on giving rural communities responsibility and enabling them to participate in the management of resources in the villagers' land area (*terroir*), with the aim of achieving more secure land tenure and sustainable resource use. The approach combines the *aménagement des terroirs*, agro-forest-pastoral production activities and the creation of socio-economic infrastructure, to achieve sustainable development at the local level (PNGT, 1995).

The *aménagement des terroirs* is defined as a process of implementing concerted action and measures for the sustainable exploitation of the natural resources in the village territory, both at the community and the individual level. *Aménagement* refers to improvement and involves a variety of investments to raise the productivity of the natural resources in a given area. The concept is used to describe a series of actions that involve using the resource in a particular way, limiting access to certain times and controlling levels of resource use.

The *gestion des terroirs* approach is broader. It calls for a rational utilisation of *all* resources of the village territory (natural, human, financial, etc.), is bottom-up, global (involving various dimensions of livelihoods), flexible and decentralised to the village level. The professionals in the field – the *Equipe Mobile Pluridisciplinaire* (EMP) – work as a multidisciplinary team, thus acknowledging the complementarity between their disciplines.

The PNGT was created as a measure to halt environmental degradation and create conditions for economic growth in rural areas. The programme is equivalent to the PGRN in Benin but, unlike the first, is a nation-wide programme. Although the PNGT is a government programme, it manages to cooperate with both international and local NGOs.

From the governmental standpoint, the problem to be dealt with was the severe degradation of the biophysical environment since 1950 and the catastrophic droughts from 1969-1973. This created fragile conditions for agricultural development in a country where 90% of the population depends on the exploitation of land and natural resources such as water, forests and pastures, for their livelihoods. A diagnosis carried out by the government (PNGT, 1995) attributed the "ecological crisis" to both physical and human factors. The first resulted from endemic droughts, which caused ecological disorders such as soil degradation, decline in annual rainfall, and the destruction of the vegetation cover. The human factors observed included demographic pressure (which leads to the reduction of fallow periods and the continually increasing exploitation of the natural resources), anarchical land clearing for shifting cultivation and herding, burning, and excessive tree cutting. Unsuitable land tenure systems (parcelling out of lands and property conflicts which lead to insecurity) were considered as critical human factors. The ecological degradation resulted in the migration of people and uncontrolled transhumance from the degraded areas. In sum, the Burkina governments had no choice but to devise measures to halt the environmental degradation and create conditions for economic growth in the rural areas.

At the local level, as in Benin, the utilisation of the villagers' land area is characterised by serious conflicts between different categories of stakeholders. Increasing drought has caused the migration of farmers and herders from the drier regions to the southern part of Burkina Faso, where the Houet province is located. In the village of Kadomba in the department of Satiri, where this study was carried out, the arrival of many migrant Mossi started in 1970, when severe droughts occurred in the Sahel. Land in Kadomba belongs to six big family compounds of the native Bobo. Within these families, the family heads have the right to give land to migrants. This prerogative is in the interest of the family heads, because the receivers of land will give many presents, such as animals, money, or cola nuts, and they will return each year to give a small present, such as chickens. As a result, many migrants received and have continued to receive land until now. Migrants do not purchase the land, but borrow it from the owner, who is supposed get it back later. The main problem perceived by the Mossi migrants is insecurity of tenure and declining soil fertility.

In addition to the native and migrant farmers, herders also live in the territory of Kadomba. Conflicts between herders and farmers started in the early 1970s, with the arrival of the first herders who stayed temporarily in the village. The herders' cattle caused serious damage to the cotton farms. The herders, in their turn, accuse the farmers of closing corridors for the cattle to pass, thus making their movement very difficult.[12] Conflicts occurred with herders living on the periphery of Kadomba as well as the transhumants. The cattle of the first group destroyed crops just after sowing, while the transhumants created trouble during harvesting, especially of cotton. The cattle also stamped the watering places used by the villagers and the women who fetch water complained about this.

In the face of these problems, the PNGT's basic approach is to replan the pasture areas into forest-pastoral zones, in which specific parts of the village territory are set aside for different sustainable uses, such as cultivated land, pastures or forests. The forest-pastoral zone should include a corridor space to facilitate the passage of cattle, watering points and animal care paddocks (*parcs de vaccination*). Tree planting in the zone is permitted, preferably with tree species the leaves of which can be used as fodder for cattle. To improve

---

[12] The strategy of the herders to cope with the environmental uncertainties is to move to the humid areas in the dry season in order to find fresh pasture. In the rainy season, it is good for the cattle's health to move to the dry area and avoid too much humidity.

the quality of pastures in the zone, the bush is to be enriched with fodder species. The carrying capacity of the zone receives particular attention through the rotation of the parcels, based on a rational utilisation of the pastures. Activities such as farming, hunting and house building are forbidden in the forest-pastoral zone. The natural resources such as trees, pastures and water need to be managed. This became part of the *gestion des terroirs* activities under the PNGT and involved:

-   making decisions on the allocation of certain parts of the village territory to livestock production and tree planting;
-   planning of activities to facilitate livestock production in this zone; and
-   defining the organisational structure to involve the stakeholders in the management.

The second objective of the PNGT was to reduce conflicts through shared understanding, negotiated agreements and concerted actions among the stakeholders.

II.6.2   Social learning and negotiation
The EMP started the creation of a forest-pastoral zone by inviting men and women from Kadomba, whether they were native Bobo, migrant Mossi or herders, to participate in village forums. These forums were organised to facilitate collective learning, so that the participating stakeholders would perceive the need to manage the forest-pastoral zone. The discussion among groups of stakeholders participating in the forum was supported by a mapping exercise, which presented a visual basis for exploring various options for reorganising the village territory. During the forums, the EMP team also collected data for a participatory rural appraisal. Collective decision making at the forums took the form of covenants among the participating stakeholders for the re-organisation of the village territory. The participants proposed to place the herders on one side of the village territory and the crop farmers on the other.

The herders did not come to the village meetings. They were unhappy about the reorganisation of the village territory. They would appreciate the creation of a forest-pastoral zone for the rainy season, the period in which there are many crop farms, but would like to go beyond this zone during the dry seasons to find pasture for their cattle.

Nor were the migrant Mossi interested in the forum for collective decision making. They feared that the reorganisation of the village territory would deprive them of the lands they had borrowed from the Bobo.

After the village forums, local plans were negotiated for the delimitation of the forest-pastoral zone and the allocation of various land uses. To assist this process, a platform was created, based on the mobilisation of existing local organisations (Box 1). Each of these organisations had their representatives in the village committee for the *gestion des terroirs* (CVGT). For issues to be negotiated and solved beyond the level of the village territory, a committee was created with representatives of each CVGT involved.

A platform for the management of a forest-pastoral zone involving the existing local organisations was expected to assist the mobilisation of local peoples' experience, to give a say to the different socio-economic groups and to stimulate a holistic view of the solution to the problems identified. It was also hoped that such a platform would avoid conflicts among the existing local organisations and promote a synergy among them in the performance of management activities.

Box 1   Local organisations represented in the platform for the management of the forest-pastoral zone

- *Groupement de Gestion Forestière* (GGF): the organisation for the exploitation of the wood lot in the Maro Forest (see Section II.5);
- *Groupement Villageois d'Agriculteurs* (GVA): the organisation of cotton and other crop farmers;
- *Groupement Villageois d'Eleveurs* (GVE): the organisation of animal (cattle, goat, sheep or pig) breeders;
- *Comité Technique Villageois* (CTV): group of villagers trained in a specific domain, such as erosion control, afforestation techniques or bee keeping;
- *Comité de Gestion du Materiel* (CGM): group of people responsible for maintaining tools and equipment brought in by the PNGT;
- *Groupement Villageois Féminin* (GVF): the women's organisation;
- *Comité Coutumier des Vieux* (CCV): the organisation of the elderly.

After the plans had been negotiated at the level of the stakeholders, the next step was the negotiation for official recognition at the provincial level. This took a considerable amount of discussion, as the plan needed to be discussed in relation to the governmental management plan. The professionals of the EMP had a mediating role here. Their task was to reconcile the management plan generated at the grassroots level with the conception of the official territorial management plan generated at the level of the province. Mediation was one way of incorporating different values and aspirations from the "bottom" to the level of development plans at the "top".

After negotiation and mediation at the province level, the EMP returned to the village to implement the management activities with the stakeholders. This involved the establishment of the boundaries of the forest-pastoral zone, fixing landmarks or painting trees to mark the boundaries, and tracing the corridor space in the zone with landmarks in cement. Some stakeholders were trained to perform these activities. The landmarks in cement were made with the locally available labour, for which 500 CFA (US\$ 0.70) per day was paid.

In addition to training, the PNGT provided advice (*conseil*) and support (*appui*), as well as financial and technical support and extension. The first activities of the intervention, the introduction of composting techniques, convinced the stakeholders in Kadomba that yield can be increased at low cost on a small plot of land and that they do not need to extend the area of their farm to achieve this.

A strong point that can be learnt from the PGNT intervention is the attempt of professionals to link grassroots development to a higher policy level. The facilitation of the management took the form of mediation between the stakeholders and actors at a higher level of social aggregation. In this case, resource management activities resulted from a negotiated agreement at a higher platform.

II.6.3 Anticipating the nature of platforms for the management of the forest-pastoral zone

The fact that herders did not participate in the village forum implied that they did not have a clear idea about the use of the forest-pastoral zone. There also was uncertainty about the role of the crop farmers after the creation of the forest-pastoral zone. Whose responsibility would it be to decide whether other herders could also use the zone? If the same idea was not developed in many other regions, the forest-pastoral zone would attract other herders. The herders would not be able to chase away these newcomers. The management of the forest-pastoral zone should therefore be the concern of both herders and crop farmers.

The management problem of the forest-pastoral zone has several dimensions. The first concerns the maintenance of the infrastructure. Users such as transhumants are not necessarily located in the village territory and making them contribute to public goods would be very difficult. In order to find a solution for the support of the infrastructure, it would be necessary to define a user group, based on a survey of the location of the herders and the size of their flocks.

The second dimension of the problem is the need for an organisation covering the many village territories of a forest-pastoral zone, in order to maintain corridor space.

Thirdly, there is the problem of allocating and regulating the use of natural resources such as water and pasture for the cattle and fuel wood. To solve this problem, the PNGT developed the idea of "carrying capacity", on the basis of which a system of rotational grazing would be developed. This could hardly be expected to work, however, as the movement of transhumants is highly unpredictable.

Solutions to the problems above can be expected to work only if they result from a learning process among all the stakeholders involved – both herders and crop farmers. This learning process should take place at the level of the forest-pastoral zone and consist of the following components:

- the development of indicators for assessing the state of natural resources, based on experimental learning, so that they will be well understood by the stakeholders;
- the development of new methods to improve the forest-pastoral zone (*e.g.* water and pasture);
- the prevention of conflicts and the development of strategies for resolving such conflicts (*e.g.* negotiated agreement and concerted action with respect to other stakeholders, such as transhumant herders).

The type of resource management in the forest-pastoral zone determines who are the stakeholders and at which level they should take concerted action (see Table 3). The forest-pastoral zone can be governed effectively only if platforms are operational at different levels.

The facilitation of change will involve new roles for the intervening agents. The transfer of competencies to local collectivities, decision-making autonomy

Table 3 Resource management activities in the forest-pastoral zone and their optimal level of effectiveness

Resource management activities in the forest-pastoral zone	The relevant stakeholders	Level of effectiveness	Comments
Maintenance of corridor space	Herders / farmers	Several village territories are concerned	Both herders and farmers have to respect the corridor space; the farmers do not cultivate there
Water use by herds and maintenance of infrastructure	Herders / farmers	Several village territories are concerned	Agreement on the rules and regulations for water use and contribution to the maintenance of infra-structure are important
Fodder cultivation for cattle	Herders	Several village territories are concerned, depending on the location of the herders	The regulation of use and exclusion of those who did not contribute should be the core issue
Tree planting and wood lot exploitation	Farmers	The village territory	When the villagers of a territory are interested in tree planting and wood exploitation

and the transfer of certain decision-making powers to the stakeholders do not mean the end of intervention. Many issues and disputes arise which surpass the competence of the stakeholders, such as the presence of transhumants who cause conflicts and wars. This suggests that the new roles of public intervention should include conflict resolution, monitoring the allocation and regulation of natural resource use and mediation in disputes among stakeholders about maintaining the forest-pastoral zone. The intervention should ensure an equitable access and control over the zone.

II.7   Conclusions

This study analysed six cases of resource management – four in Benin and two in Burkina Faso. The first one, on fishery resource management in Lake Aheme, analysed the development of the platform for the resource management of Lake Aheme from a historical perspective. It showed that the impasse in the management of the lake could be broken only if two conditions were fulfilled: effective collective action and negotiated agreement on regulation, mutual control and monitoring and a platform for governing the lake and solving conflicts, such as the one that existed in pre-colonial times. The failure to set up a new organisation among the interest groups was a factor which seriously impeded the management of Lake Aheme.

The second case study compared two situations of rangeland resource management within the Chabe community in Benin: the local arrangement in Savè and the implementation of the *appui-conseil* for collective rangeland resource management. The first situation revealed that, in spite of various local arrangements, a lack of decision-making capacity and concerted action and the absence of organisations and institutions for resource management resulted in failures. In the second situation, externally supported negotiated agreement and concerted action led to the development of a platform for collective rangeland resource management in Kemon (Collines province). The major conclusion from this study is that barriers to collective rangeland resource management can be overcome if different categories of stakeholders realise their mutual dependence, adopt collective action and develop platforms for collective decision making, monitoring sanctions and exclusion at the level of *gaa*, villages and regions. The study showed that external support and an enabling environment can play a crucial role in the social learning process which leads to effective platform development.

The third case study presented watershed problems affecting two ethnic groups, the Adja and Mahi in Benin. The critical issue here was whether the extent of scaling up watershed development from the level of the farms to the watershed for intervention purposes was effective. It implied the need

59

to develop inter-village perspectives. Within both ethnic groups, the absence of consistent property rights institutions was a barrier to watershed development. Platforms for pooling a systematic treatment of micro-watersheds towards watershed development based on inter-village structuring (scaling up) had not yet emerged in Couffo. One reason was the absence of local organisations to strengthen this process. In Ouèssè, the creation of the *Comité Inter-Villageoise pour la Gestion des Ressources Naturelles* (UIGREN), also called SEDOKU, was a platform at the level of the region of the Mahi people. The success of the scaling-up process could be attributed to existing organisations and a collective learning path adopted by the intervening agency.

Resource-flow management by a women's group to improve soil fertility was analysed in the fourth case study. The analysis considered two different contexts: before and during democratisation in Benin. It was seen that resource-flow management is effective only if successful collective action is maintained to provide public goods, such as infrastructure. A major conclusion from this study is that a shift in the political system of Benin had some effect in making grassroots development processes more dynamic. Many opportunities, such as credit, training and exchange of experiences made possible the maintenance of the group and, in turn, collective action for resource management.

The fifth case study showed the development of dealing with forestry problems from a purely indigenous regulation to the recent intervention of the PGNT and co-management practices in Burkina Faso. This case study reveals that the development of the platform is sensitive to ownership issues concerning the Maro Forest. This case involves both public goods (*e.g.* firebreaks) and common goods (*e.g.* trees). Co-management practices, the exclusion of free riders and monitoring facilitated collective action and platform development in the Maro Forest.

The *gestion des terroirs* approach employed in a physical planning context to create a zone for herding and tree planting in the Houet province (Burkina Faso) was analysed in the last case study. The main issue here was the management of a forest-pastoral zone. The need to initiate this management arose from severe problems such as crop damage caused by transhumant herders, and conflicting interests between herders, the native Bobo and migrant Mossi. The perceived interdependence between these stakeholders was a driving factor for successful collective action and the development of a platform for the management of the forest-pastoral zone. This interdependence had become visible through repeated conflicts between herders and crop farmers. This case study also revealed that the management of the forest-pastoral zone requires new roles for professionals, such as monitoring, conflict resolution and mediation.

The six case studies are illustrative of the various types of resource management problems distinguished in Section I.4.2, *i.e.* public good dilemmas, common good dilemmas, ecological and social crises and assurance problems (Table 4).

Table 4 Examples of public and common goods and the nature of resource management problems in the case studies

Case studies	Examples of public goods	Examples of common goods	Nature of the resource management problem
Lake Aheme	Institutions and organisations for the lake; collective akaja; hwédo for the group	Fish, shrimp, crab	Public good dilemma, ecological and social crises, common good dilemma, assurance problem, second-order dilemma
Rangeland	Corridor space; institutions and organisations for rangeland	Pastures, water for cattle	Social crises, public good dilemma
Watershed	Contour lines planted with *vetiver*; gullies; gallery forest; CGT[b]; UIGREN[c]	Rainfall water	Ecological crises, public good dilemma
Women's group	Infrastuctures for producing organic matter; the group itself; REDAD[d]	--	Public good dilemma, assurance problem
Maro Forest	Firebreaks; trees; GGF[e]; inter-village organisations	Trees (wood lot)	Ecological crises, public good dilemma, assurance problem
GZSP[a]	Corridor space; firebreaks; CVGT[f]; inter-*terroir* committee; fodder	Pastures, water for cattle, trees (wood lot)	Ecological crises, public good dilemma, assurance problem

a *Gestion de Zone Sylvo-Pastorale.*
b *Comité de Gestion de Terroir.*
c *Union Inter-villageoise pour la Gestion des Ressources.*
d *Reseau de Développement d'Agriculture Durable.*
e *Groupement de Gestion Forestière.*
f *Comité Villageois de Gestion de Terroir.*

The public good dilemma – the problem of free riders who benefit from public goods such as improvements or natural resource institutions without contributing to them – occurs especially in situations where the chance of being detected and punished is minimal or where the free riders believe they can get out of trouble through corruption (*e.g.* Lake Aheme). In the cases of resource-flow management and the wood lots of Maro Forest, in contrast, it was possible to monitor the contributions and exclude the free riders.

Ecological crises are perceived as a problem when they make sense to the stakeholders or seriously affect their livelihoods. Perceived ecological crises are experienced differently by various interest groups. The ecological crisis is socially constructed, as the cases of Lake Aheme, the rangeland in Benin and the forest-pastoral zone in Burkina Faso reveal.

Social crises, especially conflicts, arise when the actions of one group affect the activities and livelihoods of other groups (*e.g.* herders *vs.* farmers in the rangeland cases or xha and akaja fishers *vs.* others in the Lake Aheme study) and/or when the stakeholders fail to agree upon institutions and organisations for resource management (*e.g.* the rangeland case in Savè, Benin). The Lake Aheme study and the rangeland study in Kemon revealed the role a third party could play in mediating disputes and establishing social justice in the appropriation of common goods.

Common good dilemmas represent the failure of the market to regulate natural resource use. The Lake Aheme study showed that the common good dilemma emerges in a situation where the scarcity of common goods (fishery resources) leads to competitive arenas. The same study shows that the lack of alternative economic opportunities and degradation of livelihoods acerbate common good dilemmas.

The assurance problem is conditioned by the way stakeholders perceive the contributions of their fellows or the effectiveness of existing mechanisms for resolving resource use dilemmas. This problem emerges where sanctioning structures are loosened (*e.g.* Lake Aheme) or corruption occurs. The assurance problem becomes visible when individual stakeholders are invited to contribute financially to a collective infrastructure for resource management. The assurance problem is less important for labour contributions to collective work (*e.g.* digging gullies to protect the village mud houses against erosion, as in the Benin watershed case), as it is possible to monitor directly whether the others are contributing. In the resource-flow management study, the invisibility of the women and their limited contributions during meetings contributed to the assurance problem.

An additional problem emerged in the Lake Aheme case, *i.e.* a second-order problem. This is a phenomenon related to the removal of a resource management problem to the policy level, especially in the context of an electoral system such as Benin. Political authorities prefer to be neutral or adopt a *laisser-aller* approach because they fear that taking measures might make some stakeholders unhappy. This has implications for controlling people and for strategies for acquiring stakeholders' votes.

The case studies have shown that the most common conflicts occur:
- over common resources (*e.g.* a lake, a forest, etc.);
- between groups, when one of them is more privileged than other and this is no longer accepted by the underprivileged (*e.g.* the Lake Aheme case); and
- between groups with conflicting interests (*e.g.* between herders and farmers).

With regard to the factors affecting the success or failure of the various resource management situations (research question 2), collective action and the development of a platform for sustainable collective resource management emerged as the central issues. Possibilities for continuous institutional change, a capacity for adaptation in resource management organisation and dynamic policy contexts also appeared to be essential for adaptive resource management. These issues, as well as the question about new concepts and ideas for adaptive resource management (research question 3), will be further elaborated in Part III.

III. Discussion

III.1 Scientific relevance

III.1 The constructivist perspective of socially constructed realities
Current approaches to resource management tend to be dominated by
technical and economic perspectives, while instrumental reasoning prevails
(Röling, 1994c). Such approaches lack an effective complementary social
perspective, which can add strategic and communicative reasoning by taking
account of several issues which are omnipresent in resource use situations,
such as conflicting interests, competitive arenas, conflict resolution,
negotiation, mediation and consensus formation. The scientific relevance of
this study lies in its attempt to incorporate this social perspective.

People living in different cultures "make sense" of (*i.e.* give a meaning
to) phenomena surrounding and affecting them in various ways. Resource
management involves many different stakeholders, such as development
professionals, researchers, and policy makers, and each of them is embedded
in a social process through which reality is constructed (standards, norms,
values, etc.). They are also active in the interpretation of the world around
them. Doing research in a socially constructed reality is very complex.
How can a researcher integrate different social constructions into his or her
inquiries? This study has shown that a constructivist inquiry is the most
appropriate research method. The constructivist inquiry method starts from
the assumption that there are multiple realities, depending on sense-making
processes. To study these realities, several research approaches are combined,
such as an exploratory approach for case studies, grounded theory principles,
longitudinal in-depth investigations and comparisons between similar cases.

Instead of trying to "prove" preconceived hypotheses in an ex-post phase
of the research process by reliability and validity indicators, the present
study has constantly made use of trustworthiness and authenticity criteria
(Table 5). The main lesson from the present study is that making use of the
trustworthiness and authenticity criteria in the constructivist methodology
is a propensity which runs from the beginning to the end of a piece of

research. This lesson is visible in the way the case studies were selected, the constant check on the value systems of the stakeholders involved in an in-depth investigation, and the comparison between similar cases. Trustworthiness criteria were satisfied by looking at the historical development of the resource management situations studied and by comparing similar natural resource management topics (*e.g.* watershed development in two different eco-zones or rangeland management under local arrangement *vs.* external support). Both the historical and the comparative approach made possible the identification of factors which led (or did not lead) to successful collective action and platforms.

Authenticity criteria were satisfied by the use of participatory methodologies. Sharing space with stakeholders during participatory action research was another way to ensure authenticity criteria. Concrete examples were the mapping exercise with herders in Savè, and the matrix ranking with a women's group in Djeffa.

Table 5 Criteria for ensuring rigour (after Guba and Lincoln, 1989)

Main criteria	Trustworthiness	Authenticity
Sub-criteria	Credibility (paralleling internal validity) Transferability (paralleling external validity) Dependability (paralleling reliability) Confirmability (paralleling objectivity)	Fairness Ontological authenticity Educative authenticity Catalytic authenticity Tactical authenticity

III.1.2   A new conceptual approach to resource management

Each of the case studies drew specific conclusions about the factors that affect the success or failure of resource management. As was pointed out in the previous section, those case studies which showed relative success also showed successful collective action. Factors governing success are therefore related to the extent to which one or more platforms are developed and are functioning effectively. Factors such as a lack of decision-making capacity, inconsistent institutional and policy frameworks, and weak policy contexts increase the risk of failure in resource management. This has implications for adaptive resource management, which will be discussed below.

Firstly, this study has made clear that adaptive resource management is different from conventional technology development, in which technology transfer is the dominant practice. The concept of innovation needs to be widened to involve negotiation between wants and gains in conflicting resource management situations. Adaptive resource management involves many trade-offs, which means that what stakeholders want is not necessarily what they should get if sustainability is to be achieved. This way of thinking about innovation implies new roles for professionals, such as conflict resolution, facilitation of collective action and platform development.

Secondly, several issues emerged regarding the facilitation of adaptive resource management. These can be classified according to the following key variables: practices, facilitation of learning, support institutions and networks, and conducive policy contexts. These key variables can be used to elaborate some practical ideas about the facilitation of adaptive resource management (see Box 2 in Part IV - Recommendations).

Thirdly, the lessons from the case studies suggest that a new vision is required for the assessment of sustainability under adaptive resource management. The study showed that sustainability in relation to adaptive resource management depends on the extent to which:
- collective action is being achieved;
- resource management institutions are internalised or have become a body of community social capital in which they build trust;
- community decision-making capacity, quality of leadership, and management capacity are maintained;
- the policy context enables conditions for adaptive resource management.

III.2   Recommendations for further research
The lessons of this study suggest some ideas for further research. The following questions could be a starting point:
- How to optimise the interaction between governmental agencies, non-governmental organisations and local peoples' groups in the planning, execution and summing up of field experiments leading to collective resource management?
- How can a scaling-up process and the corresponding creation of an organisation for collective decision making, monitoring and joint learning be facilitated?
- How to enhance the effectiveness of mediation to resolve conflicts about the management of natural resources?
- How to use Geographic Information Systems (GIS) in interaction with stakeholders to make problems visible in an ecosystem, so that they can move to a shared understanding and collective action?

III.3   Practical applicability
This study has generated several lessons for resource management. They concern the inclusion of all stakeholders, the importance of social learning,

the exchange of experiences, collective action, platform development and facilitation.

Inclusion of all stakeholders
The case studies made it clear that obtaining a comprehensive view of a problem situation requires the inclusion of all stakeholders, and not only the farmers. These stakeholders perceive the situation in different ways. The xha users in the Lake Aheme case study, for instance, invoked historical and religious prerogatives as a basis for their perception of things. To understand how different stakeholders make sense of the situation is a prerequisite for any intervention to solve a problem situation. Where outsiders look at the situation solely from their own standpoint, intervention will not succeed.

The importance of social learning
The study also revealed the importance of social learning. All the case studies showed attempts to solve the conflict, though the attempts were not always successful. Where there was a effort to learn together and where the initiative to improve the situation came from the stakeholders themselves and was then supported by outsiders, the success was greater than in conflict situations where this was not the case.

Learning, in this context, does not necessarily mean learning new facts. It rather involves the reconstruction of sense making (of the ecosystem, social processes or platform development) applying relevant concepts. These often come from indigenous knowledge and are conveyed in traditional forms, such as metaphors (*e.g. yanpekpe* in the rangeland case in Kemon) or spiritism (*e.g. Dagboehounso* in the Lake Aheme case study). Intervention agencies can use these forms to promote joint learning, *e.g.* by staging performances with relevant messages or holding song contests. Other ways of social learning include:
- experimentation and observation (*e.g.* erosion control techniques in the Ouèssè watershed case study);
- dialogue (*e.g.* through field visits, network activities and excursions, such as in the women's group case study in Djeffa);
- organised interactive processes between the intervening party and the stakeholders (*e.g.* the discussion of contour farming practices in Ouèssè or the participatory mapping exercise in the watershed case study in Benin).

Interventions play a catalytic role for collective learning in resource management situations. Interventions in realising collective action and

platform development processes were successful in the case studies of the rangeland in Kemon, watershed development, the management of the forest-pastoral zone and the Maro Forest. In the watershed and the Maro Forest case studies, joint learning led to agreement on concrete actions by the intervening agency and a group of stakeholders.

Exchange of experiences
The case studies in Burkina Faso, where the intervening agency (PNGT) brought several groups together, showed that the exchange of experiences between groups who were trying to solve similar problems proved to be very helpful. Success in solving one problem creates an incentive to solve others. In the case of the Adja Plateau, for example (Section II.3), the villagers who had successfully dug a trench system to drain flood water from the village centre started to discuss the possibility of constructing an all-weather road to the village and how they could best use the runoff water. After the villagers had experienced the benefit of draining the village centre, many of them started to imitate the same practices in their fields. Thus, demonstration with encouragement of self-confidence and motivation proved to be a successful strategy.

Collective action
The forgoing already indicates that collective action is a key condition for solving resource management problems. Public good dilemmas, common good dilemmas and assurance problems can be solved only if collective action is effective (*i.e.* are the result of interaction, negotiation, mediation and conflict resolution). Ecological and social crises can be solved if the stakeholders share their understanding of the problem. Collective action means that individual action is consistent with norms, rules, etc., which are collectively agreed upon. Collective action can be expressed through the willingness of many stakeholders to act beyond their individual interest, perhaps because of stimuli from their environment.

All the case studies show that a relative success in resource management was achieved where social action was effective. Quota measures and rationing of fishery resources for the akaja practice in the Lake Aheme during the colonial period were not successful because the stakeholders did not accept collective action. Policy prerogatives for establishing social justice, equity and enabling conditions for breaking impasses around Lake Aheme did not succeed because two coalitions of stakeholders (Xha people and akaja users) did not act collectively. However, the governance of this lake had been successful when the stakeholders adopted collective action during pre-colonial times. The case of the women's group in Djeffa reveals that regenerative practices such as resource-flow management are conditioned by successful collective action and by active participation of the stakeholders to provide many public goods. Co-management practices for the Maro Forest in Burkina Faso involve successful collective action to maintain firebreaks and keep the forest from being destroyed by unexpected bush fires.

The case studies showed that the conditions for successful collective action are:
- perceived interdependence in relation to resource management (*e.g.* in the Lake Aheme case study, where stakeholders realised their interdependence when fishery resources became scarce, or in the rangeland case in Savè where the economy of villagers and herders in Ayedjoco was integrated and the herders kept the villagers' cattle);
- sharing risks in collective resource management (*e.g.* the initial problems with pig raising in the women's group case study in Djeffa);
- mutual benefits (*e.g.* in Kemon, where peace, security and business (cattle trade) created an environment for mutual benefit);
- perceived externalities within resource management activities (*e.g.* access to credit and extension in the case of the Djeffa women's group); and
- trust in social capital (institutions and organisations) for resource management (*e.g.* the rules and new rangeland management organisation of the Chabe people in Kemon). This aspect refers to the assurance problem and is a condition for maintaining successful collective action.

Platform development
Successful collective action requires the development of platforms. Examples from the case studies are the development of a platform for the management of Lake Aheme, the operational platform in Kemon in the Benin rangeland study and the platform perspective among Chabe people in the village of Ayedjoco in the Savè case study. The watershed development case study showed many platforms and demonstrated the importance of scaling up towards the whole watershed. The Maro Forest case study untangles ownership and level of management for the definition of platforms.

When the boundary is not a relevant issue for the conceptualisation of the ecosystem under siege, the effective platform for resource management does not depend on the ecosystem level. This situation applies, for instance, to the resource-flow management case study of the women's group in Djeffa. In this situation, networking at higher levels of social aggregation for a range opportunities is the most important thing.

Seven conditions for the functioning of effective platforms for resource management can be identified from the case studies:
- collective action;
- representation at the appropriate ecosystem level;
- quality of leadership;
- opportunities for meeting;
- capacity for implementing mechanisms for concerted action and conflict resolution;
- stakeholders are the main factor for the functioning of operational platforms; and
- opportunities for continual learning in order to assist adaptability.

Facilitation
Collective action and the development of effective platforms for successful natural resource management can be enhanced through facilitation. The study showed that the notion of facilitation as applied to resource management goes beyond technology transfer, advisory and information support services, and extension which focus on the solution of specific problems. Critical issues such as breaking impasses, overcoming barriers and scaling up individual actions, enlarge the horizon of facilitation in resource management.
Facilitation can focus on a deliberate process of developing or stimulating the use of a regenerative practice (*e.g.* akaja or hwédo in the Lake Aheme study or contour farming in the case of watershed development). Successful collective action and platforms can be facilitated through communicative intervention, such as *animation rurale*, non-formal education, folk media and participatory learning. Leadership promotion and the development of institutions for solving social dilemmas can be the main issues.
   A particular phenomenon noticed in the case studies is the emergence of new roles for professionals in the field. These include conflict resolution, mediation and negotiation. Serious difficulties were also noted for these emerging roles. Observations from Benin and Burkina Faso revealed that resource management activities were embedded in administrative structures where professionals work with "instructions". Moreover, high-level positions in resource management organisations are held by specialists in specific domains, *i.e.* foresters, fishery specialists, vets, etc. Existing conditions therefore do not permit these new roles to be fully exploited. Recently, multidisciplinary teams have emerged at the lower level of organisations' hierarchy. Professionals involved at this level are mostly targeted for training programmes in the use of communicative strategies (participatory methodologies to stimulate changes). Lessons from the case studies reveal

that professionals at the higher levels of organisations' structures must also be targeted, so that they can learn to adopt communicative behaviour to pool efforts for negotiated agreements, concerted action, joint decision making, etc.

A flexible and supportive context
Possibilities for continuous institutional change, a capacity for adaptation in resource management organisation and dynamic policy contexts are also essential for adaptive resource management. Institutions and organisations for resource management, be they governmental or non-governmental, should be capable of adapting locally in line with changing conditions. This requires policies which make possible the transfer of certain decision-making powers (statutory or regulatory) to the local level. A key word here is "decentralisation", *i.e.* conditions to facilitate the creation of local political entities to debate resource management problems and alternative solutions at the community level.

To sum up, the case studies suggest that intervention in a problem situation can be successful if:
-   the local people share a common understanding of the problem and realise that they have to be the major bearer of the task, in which the intervention agents can only assist;
-   decisions are made on a platform, on which all the stakeholders are represented;
-   the representatives can count on the support and acceptance of the decisions by their constituent group;
-   the analysis of the problem, the devising of possible solutions and the final decision making are based on joint learning and comprehension and collective action; and
-   the participatory approach is supported at the policy level.

IV. Recommendations

The following recommendations for development making use of adaptive resource management are suggested:

1. Intervention can be helpful and is often needed; but it should emphasise facilitation and mediation rather than law enforcement. When governmental, non-governmental and grassroots (people's) organisations pool their efforts (as in the Burkina Faso case) the relative advantages of each can lead to an optimisation of the outcome. Some practical ideas about interventions in adaptive resource management are summarised in Box 2.

2. Decision making on adaptive management of natural resource goods should be decentralised and delegated to the relevant ecosystem level, *e.g.* natural regions, watersheds and village territories, and not to administrative units which are often artificial in former colonial countries. To make possible this change in attitude, decision makers and those in charge of implementation at the centre of power need "training" and encouragement in rethinking their roles in the development process. The *terroir* as a planning and implementation unit should become better known in the anglophone world and adapted to local conditions.

3. Natural resource management involves the need to resolve conflicts about the use of commonly owned resources. To seek solutions to these conflicts, platforms have to be established and further developed at the appropriate level, on which all stakeholders can meet and discuss different views. Helping local organisations to become more effective enhances their chances of representing the interests of their members on such platforms and ensuring that their constituents will accept the outcome of the joint decision making.

Box 2 Practical ideas about interventions in adaptive natural resource management

1. *Practices that underpin adaptive resource management*
   - promoting individual actions which are consistent with the collective goal at the ecosystem level;
   - taking less from common goods (especially in situations of complex arenas and natural resource scarcity);
   - giving more to public goods, be they organisations, institutions, infrastructures, etc.;
   - sharing understanding of the ecosystem to resolve social and ecological crises;
   - fostering organisational development to counter assurance problems and second order dilemmas.

2. *Learning in adaptive resource management*
   - accepting multiple perspectives;
   - learning to think at the level of ecosystem under siege;
   - learning to reach agreement through negotiation, mediation and interaction;
   - creating opportunities for reflexive learning by stakeholders;
   - developing opportunities for non-formal education or *animation rurale*.

3. *Facilitation of learning*
   - using soft system methodology to create a rich picture in problem situations;
   - using RAAKS (Rapid Appraisal for Agricultural Knowledge Systems) for identifying the mission statements of various intervening agencies;
   - using Stakeholders Analysis to make trade-offs visible in solutions;
   - organising learning paths to demonstrate mutual interdependence;
   - creating conditions for discovery learning;
   - using a process approach to encouraging the acceptance of responsibility;
   - organising a structuring process for platform development;
   - promoting leadership to make platforms effective;
   - linking platform to higher levels of social aggregation;
   - using RAAKS for role development among various intervening agencies;
   - training stakeholders, transferring competencies and training local trainees;
   - creating incentives to stimulate successful collective action.

4. *Support institution and networks*
   - using platforms for adaptive resource management at the appropriate ecosystem level;
   - networking with various governmental or non-governmental organisations to perform various activities within resource management;
   - using learning groups and stakeholders organisations;
   - defining property right institutions for adaptive resource management;
   - defining rules of use and covenants to monitor their implementation;
   - defining rules for exclusion and designing sanctions structures;
   - using existing local organisations for adaptive resource management.

5. *Conducive policy context*
   - decentralising certain powers to the grass-roots levels;
   - supporting learning communities in collective resource management;
   - reforming external research and development organisations to become activists at the grassroots level;
   - supporting regulations to counter "market failure" in resource use;
   - adopting mechanisms for long-term planning with communities.

4. Fostering local self-organisation, establishing local meeting places, using local media and facilitating transport of local groups to visit other groups to study similar problems, should be enhanced. Local community leaders, especially promising youngsters, should be trained in organisational skills. Meeting other groups and facilitators should enhance the joint learning process which is needed to combine experiences of the past with new opportunities.

5. Governments should have the courage to forbid, by laws and other means, practices that endanger the sustainability of ecosystems, such as small mesh size of fishing nets, excessive tree cutting for farming and the overuse of common goods.

References

Adjinacou, C. Aho, J. Agbo, E. (1995). *Rapport annuel Janv.-Dec. 1995. PGRN, volet ABV/GT*. Quèssè (Bénin): GERAN/PGRN.

Berreman, G.D. (1972). *Hindus of the Himalayas: ethnography and change*. Berkeley: University of California Press.

Billaz, R. and Diawara, Y. (1981). *Enquête en milieu rural Sahélien*. Paris: ACCT, PUF.

Brccmer, H.P.M., Bergh, R.R. and Hesseling, G. (1995). 'Towards local management of natural resources in Senegal', in J.P.M. van den Breemer, C.A. Drijver and L.B. Venema (eds.) *Local resource management in Africa*. Chichester: John Wiley & Sons.

Bruyn, T.S. (1966). *The human perspective in sociology: the methodology of participant observation*. New Jersey: Prentice-Hall, Inc.

Checkland, P.B. (1981). *System thinking, system practice*. Chichester: John Wiley and Sons.

Conway, G.R. (1986). *Agroecosystem analysis for research and development*. Bangkok: Winrock International.

Conway, G.R. (1994). 'Sustainability in agricultural development. Trade-offs between productivity, stability, and equitability'. *Journal of Farming Systems Research Extension* 4(2): 1-14.

Costanza, R. and C. Folke (1996). 'The structure and function of ecological systems in relation to property-rights regime', in S. Hanna, C. Folke and K.G. Mäler (eds.) *Rights to nature: ecological, economic, cultural, and political principles of institutions for the environment*. Washington, D.C.: Island Press.

Dangbégnon, C. (1998). *Platforms for resource management. Case studies of success or failure in Benin and Burkina Faso*. PhD thesis Wageningen Agricultural University.

Dawes, R.M. (1980). 'Social dilemmas'. *Annual Review of Psychology* 31: 169-93.

Doolette, J.B. and William, B.M. (eds.) (1990*). Watershed development in Asia. Strategies and technologies*. World Bank Technical Paper 127. Washington, D.C.: The World Bank.

Engel, P. (1997). *The social organization of innovation. A focus on stakeholder interaction.* Amsterdam: Royal Tropical Institute.

Equipe Mobile Pluridisciplinaire du Houet (1996). *Bilan des activités (1992 B 1996) et perspectives.* Ouagadougou: Programme National de Gestion des Terroirs.

Fairhead, J. (1991). 'Indigenous technical knowledge and natural resource management in sub-Saharan Africa: a critical overview'. Paper of the National Resource Institute, Chatham (UK).

Fresco, L.O. (1986). *Cassava in shifting cultivation. A system approach to agricultural technology development in Africa.* Amsterdam: Royal Tropical Institute.

Glaser, B.G. and Strauss, A.L. (1967). *The discovery of grounded theory. Strategies for qualitative research.* Chicago: Aldine Publishing Company.

Groot, R.S. de (1992). *Functions of nature.* Groningen: Wolters-Noordhoff.

Guba, R. and Lincoln, Y.S. (1989). *Fourth generation evaluation.* London: Sage Publication.

Hardin, G. (1968). 'The tragedy of the commons'. *Science* 162: 1243-1248.

INSAE (1993). *Deuxième recensement général de la population et de l'habitation, Fevr. 1992. Vol. 1, Résultats définitifs.* Cotonou: Ministère du Plan et de la Restructuration Economique.

McCall, G.J. and Simmons, J.L. (eds.) (1969). *Issues in participant observation: a text and reader.* Reading Massachusetts: Addison-Wesley Publishing Company.

McCay, B.J. and Acheson, J.M. (1987). 'Human ecology of the commons', in B.J. McCay and J.M. Acheson (eds.) *The question of the commons: the culture and ecology of communal resources.* Tucson: University of Arizona Press.

McKean, M. (1992). 'Success on the commons'. *Journal of Theoretical Politics* 4(3): 247-281.

Ninan, K.N. (1998). *An assessment of European-aided watershed development projects in India from the perspective of poverty reduction and the poor.* CDR Working Paper 98.3. Copenhagen: CDR.

Olson, M. (1978). *La logique de l'action collective.* Paris: PUF.

Onibon, P. and Okou, Ch. (1995). *Etude sur la gestion de la transhumance et des colons agriculteurs dans le bassin versant de la Beffa (Ouèssè). Projet de gestion ressources naturelles (PGRN) volet Amenagement des Bassins Versants composante operations foncieres. Rapport de consultation.* Cotonou: GERAM/PGRN.

Ostrom, E. (1990). *Governing the commons. The evolution of institutions for collective action.* Cambridge: University Press.

Peacock, J.L. (1986). *The anthropological lens: harsh light, soft focus.* Cambridge: Cambridge University Press.

Pelto, P.J. and Pelto, G.H. (1978). *Anthropological research: the structure of the inquiry.* Cambridge: Cambridge University Press.

Pliya, J. (1980). *La pêche au Sud-Ouest du Bénin. Etude de géographie appliquée sur la pêche continentale et maritime.* Paris: ACCT.

Programme National de Gestion de Terroir (1995). *Les grandes orientations en matière de gestion des terroirs au Burkina Faso, deuxième version.* Ouagadougou: Ministère de l'Agriculture et des Ressources Animales.

Rap, E. (1997). *Preparing exploratory research. A guideline for the design of a research proposal for MAKS students.* Wageningen: Wageningen Agricultural University.

Röling, N. (1994a). 'Platforms for decision making about eco-systems', in L.O. Fresco *et al.* (eds.) *Future of the land: mobilising and integrating knowledge for land use options.* Chichester: John Wiley and Sons.

Röling, N. (1994b). 'Creating human platforms to manage natural resources: first results of a research programme', in *Proceedings of the international symposium on systems oriented research in agriculture and rural development,* Montpellier, France, 21 - 25 November 1994.

Röling, N. (1994c). 'Communication support for sustainable natural resource management'. *IDS Bulletin* 25(2): 125-133.

Röling, N. (1996). 'Towards interactive agricultural science'. *Journal of Agricultural Education and Extension* 2(4): 35-46.

Röling, N. (1997). 'The soft side of land. Socio-economic sustainability of land use systems'. Invited paper for the Conference on Geo-Information for Sustainable Land Management, held at the International Institute for Aerospace Survey and Earth Sciences (ITC), Enschede, the Netherlands, 17-21 August, 1997. Published in *ITC Journal*, Special Congress Issue on Geo-Information for Sustainable Land Management, Vol. 1997(3-4): 248-262.

Röling, N. and J. Jiggins (1998). 'The ecological knowledge system', in N. Röling and A. Wagemakers (eds.). *Facilitating sustainable agriculture: participatory learning and adaptive management in times of environmental uncertainty.* Cambridge: Cambridge University Press.

Schelhaas, R.M. (1978). *Les sols à vocation horticole du Sud-Est du Bénin et leur fumure à la gadoue.* Amsterdam: Royal Tropical Institute.

Sen, A.K. (1967). 'Isolation, assurance and the social rate of discount'. *Quarterly Journal of Economics* 81: 112-24.

Sloep, B.P. (1994). 'The impact of "sustainability" on the field of environmental science', in G. Skirbekk (ed.) *The notion of sustainability and its normative implications.* Oslo: Scandinavian University Press.

Strauss, A. and Corbin, J. (1990). *Basics of qualitative research. Grounded theory procedures and techniques*. Newbury: Sage Publication.

Tiffen, M. and Mortimore, M. (1992). 'Environment, population growth and productivity in Kenya: a case study of Machakos District'. Draft for Development Policy Review.

Wade, R. (1988). *Village republics: economic conditions for collective action in South India*. Cambridge: Cambridge University Press.

Warren, M.D. (1991). *Using indigenous knowledge in agricultural development*. World Bank Discussion Papers 127. Washington D.C.: World Bank.

White, A. and Runge, C.F. (1994). 'Common property and collective action: lessons from cooperative watershed management in Haiti'. *Economic Development and Cultural Change* 43(1): 1-41.

Appendix 1

Participating researchers and institutions

1. Principal researchers:

Prof. (em.) Dr. Abraham Blum (project coordinator)
Hebrew University of Jerusalem
Faculty of Agriculture, Food and Environmental Quality Sciences
The Hebrew University of Jerusalem
P.O. Box 12
Rehovot 76100
Israel
Phone: 972-8-9489316/972-3-9581821
Fax: 972-8-9473305 / 972-3-9581774
e-mail: blum@agri.huji.ac.il

Dr. Constant Dangbégnon
04 BP 1386
Cotonou
Benin
Tel. (Cell.) 229-05 85 07
E-mail: cdangbe@beninweb.org
         cdangbegnon@hotmail.com

Prof. Dr. Niels Röling
Wageningen University
Department of Communication and Innovation Studies
Hollandseweg 1
6706 KN Wageningen
The Netherlands
Phone: 31-488-451016
Fax: 31-317-484791
E-mail: n.roling@inter.nl.net

Dr. Ir. Rigobert C. Tossou
National University of Benin
Faculty of Agronomic Sciences
P.O. Box 8033
Cotonou
Benin
Phone: 229-360126
Fax : 229-313559/300276
E-mail: ctossou@syfed.bj.refer.org

2. Junior researcher:

Ir. Suzanne Nederlof (socio-economist)
p/o Gijbelandsedijk 84
2974 VE Brandwijk
The Netherlands
Tel. 00 31 184 641288
E-mail: suzannenederlof@hotmail.com

3. Others:

Members of the Hebrew University's team:
G. Reshef
Ms. O. Ardon
R. Brill

Appendix 2

Follow-up of the project: capacity building and project-related publications

A major goal of this research was to enhance the research capacity of the *Université Nationale du Bénin* (UNB). This was realised in various ways. Firstly, one of its recent PhDs, Dr. Ir. Rigobert C. Toussou, was appointed to manage the local part of the research. Secondly, the project enabled Constant Dangbégnon to earn his PhD degree on the basis of this study. Both researchers participated in a seminar which was held on occasion of the NIRP Steering Committee meeting in Accra. This meeting, to which researchers from three West African projects were invited, made it possible to implement the plan for a regional symposium on agricultural knowledge systems. The major objective of this seminar, which was planned from the beginning as part of this project, was to exchange information and experience among West African researchers. This, too, has contributed to the strengthening of the research capacity of African universities.

Publications:
Danbégnon, C. (1999). 'Managing watersheds in Benin', in M.C. Monroe (ed.) *What works. A guide to environmental education and communication projects for practitioners and donors.* Washington D.C.: Academy for Educational Development / Gabriola Island: New Society Publishers.
Dangbégnon, C. (1998). *Platforms for resource management. Case studies of success or failure in Benin and Burkina Faso.* PhD thesis Wageningen Agricultural University.
Dangbégnon, C. (1999). 'Rural development in the western part of the sous-préfecture of Ouèssè', in L. Hoefsloot (ed.) *Land use planning and negotiating platforms.* The Hague: The Dutch Ministry of Foreign Affairs.
Dangbégnon, C. (1996). 'Watershed development with indigenous people in Benin'. Paper presented at the international workshop on 'Using Communication to Make Environmentally Sustainable Development Happen', 1-2 November, 1996, Burlingame, California (USA).

Dangbégnon, C. (1996). 'Breaking the impasse: platforms for common property resource use (the Aheme Lake case, Benin)'. Paper presented at the Sixth Annual Conference for the International Association for the Study of Common Property Resources, 4-8 June 1996, University of Berkeley, California (USA).

Dangbégnon, C. (1995). 'L'importance des connaissances endogènes pour une agriculture durable au Sud-Bénin', in P. Ton and L. de Haan (eds.) *A la recherche de l'agriculture durable du Bénin*. Amsterdamse Sociaal-Geografische Studies 49. Amsterdam: Instituut voor Sociale Geografie.

Dangbégnon, C., Röling, N. and Blum, A. (1995). 'New perspective on complex environmental problems in Bénin: platforms for resource use negotiation'. Paper presented at the International Congress on Agrarian Questions, Wageningen 22-24 May 1995, the Netherlands.

Maarleveld, M. and Dangbégnon, C. (1999). 'Managing natural resources: a social learning perspective'. *Agriculture and Human Values* 16: 267-280.

Nederlof, E.S. (1997). 'Facilitation of forest management. The case of wood exploitation in the classified forest of Maro, Burkina Faso. MSc Thesis Wageningen Agricultural University.

Röling, N. (1994). 'Platforms for decision making about eco-systems', in L.O. Fresco *et al.* (eds.) *Future of the land: mobilising and integrating knowledge for land use options*. Chichester: John Wiley and Sons Ltd.

Röling, N. (1994). 'Creating human platforms to manage natural resources: first results of a research programme', in *Proceedings of the International Symposium on Systems Oriented Research in Agriculture and Rural Development*, Montpellier, France, 21 - 25 November 1994, pp. 391-395.

List of members of the Joint Steering Committee

Israel:

Prof. V. Azarya (co-chair)
Dept. of Sociology and Social Anthropology
Hebrew University
Jerusalem

Prof. E. Ben-Rafael
Dept. of Sociology and Anthropology
Tel Aviv University
Tel Aviv

Prof. R.E. Isralowitz
Hubert H. Humphrey Institute for
Social Ecology
Ben-Gurion University of the Negev
Beer-Sheva

Dr. N. Trostler-Buganim
School of Nutritional Sciences
Faculty of Agriculture
Hebrew University
Rehovot

The Netherlands:

Prof. B. de Gaay Fortman (co-chair)
Institute of Social Studies
The Hague

Prof. A.J. Dietz
AGIDS (Amsterdam Research Institute for
Global Issues and Development Studies)
University of Amsterdam
Amsterdam

Prof. L.W. Nauta
formerly: Dept. of Social Philosophy and Ethics
University of Groningen

Dr. E.B. Zoomers
Centre for Latin America Research and Documentation (CEDLA)
University of Amsterdam
Amsterdam

Other titles in the NIRP Research for Policy Series

1. Bird-David, N., Karugu, W., Oduol, M. and Wandibba, S. (2000). Technological change and rural third world women: an impact study in Machakos District, Eastern Kenya. ISBN 90 6832 662 7.

2. Felsenstein, D., Foeken, D., Muraya, A. and Schwartz, D. (2000). Small-scale enterprises in rural Kenya: constraints and perspectives. ISBN 90 6832 663 5.

3. Ajaegbu, H.I., Grossman, D., Berg, L. van den (2000). Market gardening, urban development and income generation on the Jos Plateau, Nigeria. ISBN 90 6832 664 3.

4. Helman, A., Vermeer, E. and Xiaoshan, Z. (2000). The shareholding cooperative system in China. ISBN 90 6832 665 1.

5. Munene, J. and Schwartz, S. (2000). Cultural values and development in Uganda. ISBN 90 6832 666 X.

6. Spolsky, B., Tushyeh, H., Amara, M. and Bot, K. (2000). Languages in Bethlehem: the sociolinguistic transformation of a Palestinian town. ISBN 90 6832 667 8.

7. Abu-Saad, I. and Mburu, J. (2001). The influence of settlement on substance use and abuse among nomadic populations in Israel and Kenya. ISBN 90 6832 668 6.

8. Degen, A.A., Nunow, A., Zaal, A.F.M., Otieno, D.A. and Hoorweg, J.C. (2001). Market dependence of pastoralists in Kenya and Israel. ISBN 90 6832 669 4.

9. Wondimu, H. (2001). Ethnic identity, stereotypes and psychological modernity in Ethiopian young adults: identifying the potential for change. ISBN 90 6832 670 8.

10. Dangbégnon, C., Blum, A., Nederlof, E.S., Röling, N. and Tossou, R.C. (2001) Platforms for sustainable natural resource management: the case of West Africa. ISBN 90 6832 671 6.